Ways to live
in harmony
with nature

KAMALJIT K. SANGHA

Ways to Live in Harmony with Nature
Published by Kamaljit K. Sangha

First published by Classic Author and Publishing Services Pty Ltd

First published 2015

Editor: Julie Athanasiou
Designer / typesetter: WorkingType Studio (www.workingtype.com.au)

National Library of Australia Cataloguing-in-Publication entry

Creator: Sangha, Kamaljit, author.
Title: Ways to live in harmony with nature / Dr. Kamaljit Sangha ;
                edited by Julie Athanasiou.
ISBN: 9780994183774 (paperback)
Subjects: Sustainable living.
                Environmentalism.
Other Creators/Contributors:
                Athanasiou, Julie, editor.
Dewey Number: 640

Dr Kamaljit Sangha

Dr Kamaljit Sangha is an ecological economist. She works mainly in the field of ecology while applying economics to the various services and benefits of our natural systems in terms of their contribution to human wellbeing. She completed her PhD from Central Queensland University in 2004, and since then she has worked in various roles (a Natural Resource Economist, Lecturer and as a Research Fellow) at James Cook University, University of Southern Queensland, and lately, at Charles Darwin University, Darwin, NT. She has worked extensively with the Indigenous communities in north Queensland where she learnt the intricate relationships between people and their natural environment, and the importance of natural systems in people's wellbeing. Growing up on an agricultural property in India, in a cohesive community, plays a significant role in her ways of thinking. She believes this kind of holistic understanding on natural and social systems is required for all of us to connect ourselves with Mother Nature and to lead a balanced life.

*I dedicate this book to all nature lovers who
already contribute or are willing to contribute by bringing a
change in their living to improve our natural resources.*

Contents

Contents

1

Nature and us

When the Dalai Lama was asked what surprised him about humanity the most, he replied:

Man. Because he sacrifices his health in order to make money. Then he sacrifices money to recuperate his health. And then he is so anxious about the future that he does not enjoy the present; the result being that he does not live in the present or the future; he lives as if he is never going to die, and then dies having never really lived.

In the modern world, our main goal is often to accumulate material wealth, making us work hard to achieve commodities while isolating ourselves from our mind and our surroundings. In this race for material wealth, we often explore our external world but not our internal world. We do not realise what we need and do not need, what our main purpose in life is and how we can lead a 'balanced life'. By a 'balanced life,' I mean one in harmony with our social, economic and ecological environment. In this book, I deal with these three aspects and analyse how each plays a role in developing a holistic approach to living in harmony with nature.

To live a life that is ecologically sustainable and matches our economic aspirations can be a difficult proposition. However, it's perfectly possible to match our economic and ecological aspirations. My ideal is to lead a life where I work with passion while meeting the main needs of my life. In reality, like most people, I do have to work hard within the system constraints to live sustainably and to feed and raise my family. So the most important question to me, and the one that I'll be exploring in this book is how do I lead a balanced life from a socio-economic as well as an ecological perspective?

I admire the idea put forward by Amartya Sen (1999) in his book *Development As Freedom*, which says, 'people lead the lives the way they want to lead'. This idea entails all aspects of our living — social, economic, ecological, health, spiritual and cultural. This means that as a citizen of a 'developed' nation, we have the opportunity to lead our lives as we want. We have the ideal situation to understand and appreciate development and to realise how significant it could be in making us both better individuals and a better society as a whole.

However, we often misunderstand the term 'development'. We consider development means mainly 'material wealth' or to access materials and related services. Indeed, we do not develop our thinking that development is beyond materials/commodities, it's about our capabilities, and us, that is, building our capacities to lead a good life. To be a 'developed' citizen of planet Earth, we should enhance our capabilities to lead creative and healthy lives to live sustainably without becoming a burden on Earth. Rather, we trap our minds in commodities and limit ourselves to this narrow definition of development. Even though we fulfill our economic needs for food and shelter that provides us with a comfortable life, we still do not feel satisfied. There is always something lacking in our lives. This is particularly true in the developed world where we seem to be missing some pieces of the puzzle, which prevent us from living life to its fullest capacity. Herein, I am talking about a person who wants to live a satisfied life in harmony with nature.

I am particularly interested in a kind of living that is ecologically sustainable, socially acceptable and economically viable. We can think of Earth as our 'one and only house' — a house that has been spoiled and exploited to meet our needs. As we feel the

2

impacts of environmental catastrophes, we must recognise that our only house, Earth, is in danger. We must all want to save this precious house. This brings a few simple questions to my mind:

1. How can we save our home while living in the contemporary world where material wealth and comforts have become the main goals of our living?
2. How can we live in harmony with nature while carrying on our normal duties and meeting our needs for food, shelter and other comforts?
3. How can we practise living in a sustainable way that minimises our impact on the planet's natural resources?
4. How can we merge environmentally-friendly ways of living into our daily busy routine?
5. How do we balance the socio-economic and environmental (natural) perspectives of our lives?
6. How do we change our attitudes and perspectives so we can live a balanced life in harmony with nature?

At the 66th session, the United Nations (UN) General Assembly adopted a resolution on Harmony with Nature (A/RES/66/204). The UN General Assembly held a dialogue at their New York headquarters to examine how human activity has damaged Earth's natural systems and affected the planet's regenerative capacity, and how we can shift from a self-centered to an Earth-centred approach. The dialogue emphasised that our success and wealth must be measured by the balance we create between ourselves and the world around us, that is, by our ability to live in harmony with nature. Re-balancing with nature, recognising the role of Mother Earth in our socio-economic fabric and re-shaping the economy were the main points suggested to move nations forward with sustainable futures.

To shift ourselves to an Earth-centred approach, we need to explore our connections with Mother Nature. This further leads us to the main question posed in the Assembly: 'How to live in harmony with nature?' (UN, General Assembly reports A/66/302 and A/RES/66/204). This book aims to address this question at both the individual and societal level.

The UN-General Secretary submitted a report in 2011 on 'Sustainable Development — Harmony with Nature' (A/66/302). The report reflects on the relationship humans have had with the Earth, as well as with their own existence, across different stages of civilisation, from ancient times to the twenty-first century. It also proposes some relevant lessons that can be learned from ancient civilisations on connections with nature:

1. Eastern traditions (Indian and some other Asian countries) usually have no divide between the creator and his created animals. In Indian religions (Hinduism, Sikhism, Buddhism and others), there is a focus on metaphysics and the belief that our bodies are made of five elements: earth, water, air, fire and the soul. It also emphasises the concepts of *samsara* (reincarnation), *karma* (cosmic justice or the deeds we do), *moksha/mukti* (liberation from the cycle of existence) and *atma* (soul/inner ultimate reality). It preaches about good deeds that include caring for Mother Nature and other living organisms created by God.

    The Vedic philosophy of India has always emphasised the human connection with nature. Vedism is a way of life based on scriptures called Vedas/Aranyakas or 'forest books', which were written by sages who lived in the forest. The Vedas, Upanishads, Puranas and Smriti contain some of the earliest messages on ecological balance and the need for humans' ethical treatment of nature. There are strong connections suggested between stability in nature and human existence. This philosophy emphasises harmony with nature and recognises that all natural elements hold divinity.

In Chinese traditions, external nature is never understood on its own terms. It is always intimately related to human life. Chinese culture believes that reality consists of countless manifestations of one unbroken continuum, the tao. It has a cosmological myth in which the universe is viewed as an organic system of interdependent parts, thus representing a holistic perspective of life on Earth.

2. Ancient Egyptians worshiped a number of deities that involved their natural environment. They recognised the vital links between humans, nature and the divine. The fact the Nile River served their lands to produce food was deeply embedded in their rituals and belief systems. As the Nile flowed north, the ancient Egyptians believed the sun rose on one side of the river and set on the other and passed through the underworld to begin the cycle again the next day. The bright star called Sirius announced the annual floods, which brought irrigation and crop-enriching silt. This marker of time, crucial in the ancient calendar's development around 5,000 years ago, provided a cyclical background to life's rhythms.

3. In African communities, natural phenomena were once perceived to possess spiritual powers, and the natural world that supplied food and shelter was respected and revered. Certain trees were considered God's trees, sacred and endowed with healing powers. Land belonged to clans consisting of the living, the dead, and even the unborn, a concept that enhanced the idea of sharing and caring for nature.

4. Pre-Columbian cultures used the term 'Pachamama' for Mother Earth throughout the Andes. Pachamama means 'fertile and fruitful mother', and conveys the symbiosis between humankind and nature.

5. In Western traditions, Romans had specific laws for the common use of air, water and fish, as mentioned in the

Justinian Code (A.D. 529). This code represents the first body of law related to the environment and asserted that the laws of nature pertain to all life forms.

Around the world, ancient civilisations have a rich history of understanding the symbiotic connection between human beings and nature. Ancient sites, many of which UNESCO (United Nations Educational, Scientific and Cultural Organisation) has recognised as part of the World Heritage, have a part to play in twenty-first century people's spiritual, cultural and material lives.

There is evidence in ancient times that the over-use of resources by some civilisations contributed to their demise. History also provides us with evidence of cases where civilisations lost their balance with nature and vanished (mainly due to a scarcity of resources). For example, Mesopotamian and Mayan civilisations faced problems of water logging and water siltation and later vanished due to the scarcity of water resources for human use (Redman 1999, cited in *World Resources 2000–2001*, and later in 2010–11). Similarly, Harappan civilisation disappeared because of siltation and the over-use of land resources.

The World Resources report of 2000–2001 highlighted some links of more recent times (Table 1.1):

Table 1.1: History of use and misuse of resources in ancient times (Source: *World Resources Report 2000–2001***).**

1800	Australia and New Zealand *Loss of biodiversity and proliferating invasive species in island ecosystems.*	There were no hooved animals in Australia and New Zealand before Europeans arrived at the end of the 18th century and began importing them. Within 100 years, there were millions of sheep and cattle. The huge increase in grazing animals killed off many of the native grasses that were not well adapted to intensive grazing. Island biodiversity worldwide suffered some of the most dramatic losses after non-native plants and animals were introduced. Island flora and fauna had developed in isolation over millennia, and thus lacked natural predators. Many island bird species, for example, were flightless and became easy prey for invaders. It is estimated that 90 per cent of all bird extinctions occurred on islands.
1800	North America *Conversion, loss of habitat, and unrestrained killing of wildlife in North America.*	As land was cleared for settlement and cultivation around the world, animal habitats of almost every kind were reduced; animals were killed for food, hides or recreation as commerce spread. In North America, herds of bison, totaling perhaps as many as 50 million, were hunted to near extinction by the end of the 19th century. Aquatic as well as terrestrial species became targets of exploitation and extinction. In the 19th century, whales were killed in large numbers to support industrialising economies in need of whale oil in great quantity, mainly for lighting lubricants. On the northwest coast of North America, whale populations were on the verge of extinction by the 20th century.

| 1800–1900 | Germany and Japan *Industrial chemical poisoning of freshwater systems.* | The industrial revolution had a profound impact on the waters of the world. Rivers that ran through industrial zones, like the Rhine in Germany, or rivers that ran through mining zones, like the Watarase in Japan, became heavily polluted in the 19th century. The German chemical industry poisoned the Rhine so badly that salmon, which had been plentiful as late as 1765, were rare by 1914. Japan's most important copper mine in the 1800s dumped mine tailings in the Watarase River, and sulfuric acid from smelters contaminated the water and killed thousands of hectares of forest trees and vegetation. Fish and fowl died, and local residents became sick. The human birth rate dipped below the death rate in the nearby town of Ashio in the 1890s. |
| 1900 | United States and Canada *Soil erosion and loss of biodiversity in the United States and Canada.* | The Great Plains of the United States and Canada were ploughed in the late 19th and early 20th centuries and planted with new forms of drought-resistant wheat. Once the protective original grass cover was destroyed, drought in the 1930s enabled high, persistent wind storms to blow away much of the dry soil. Soil conservation methods were subsequently introduced so that when wind erosion again affected the area in the 1950s and in the 1970s the consequences were less severe. |

1928– present	Worldwide *Industrial chemicals deplete the world's protective ozone layer.*	Chlorofluorocarbons (CFCs) are a family of volatile compounds invented in 1928. Thought to be the world's first non-toxic, nonflammable refrigerants, their use grew rapidly. They also were used as industrial solvents, foaming agents and aerosol propellants. CFC production peaked in 1974, the same year researchers noted CFC emissions could possibly damage human health and the ozone layer. In 1985, the discovery of an 'ozone hole' over the Antarctic coincided with a first-ever coordinated international effort to phase out production of CFCs and other ozone-depleting substances.

In the past, humans have faced many environmental challenges such as soil degradation, salinisation, the loss of biodiversity and primary cropland, and more recently, the changes in climate. Indeed, climate change is a major challenge that we are facing as a global community in the modern time. In the past 20–30 years, we have seen a number of catastrophic events including flooding, cyclones, bushfires, heatwaves, etc., that have impacted the lives of many people at local and regional scales. Such instances teach us the important lesson that if we want to sustain ourselves on this planet, we need to live in harmony with nature. There are many examples from which we can draw wisdom, such as some long-established indigenous beliefs and traditions that, within different contexts and structures, have formed the basis for a life in harmony with nature. The 'holistic vision' inherent in all indigenous belief systems and the importance given to constant communion with nature is perhaps a key lesson.

Australian Indigenous cultures, which have survived for approximately 50,000 to 60,000 years on a dry continent, are particularly important to mention here. Their communion with nature involves physical, spiritual and human living (Fig. 1). The people's lives within these cultures involve intricate connections between their sacred, physical and social worlds, which includes connections to land, water and other natural resources. Indigenous 'oneness' with nature is clearly evident in their traditional system for 'bush tucker', rituals, totems and the kinship system that involves caring for nature's different components.

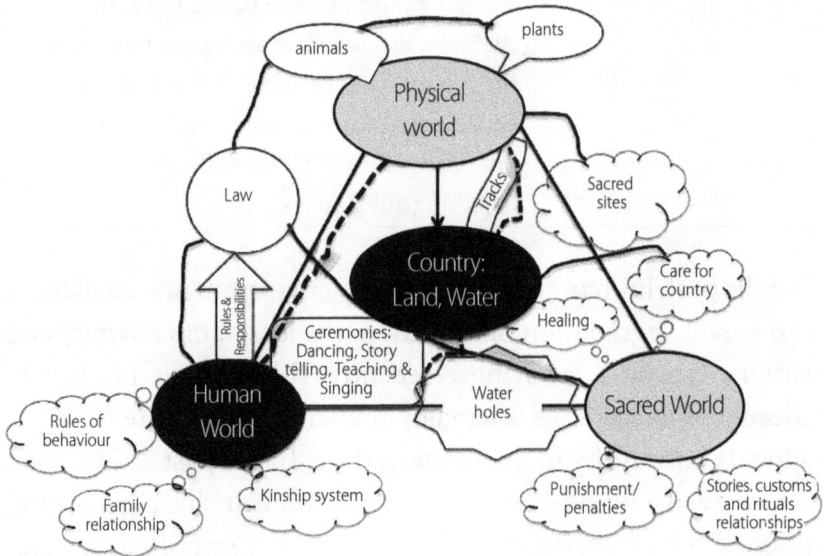

Fig. 1:   Australian Indigenous worldview
(as comprehended by the author).

Traditional Indigenous Australians consider land as the 'Mother' and care for it with responsibility. In the past, their lives were closely connected to the land and other natural resources. Most of their spiritual, social, religious and political needs were fulfilled by connecting to the land and by associating with the natural environment. Most importantly, people cared for the land not only physically, but spiritually as well. The presence of various plants and animals are also important in people's relationships, songlines, stories and ceremonies in connection with their country. Many ceremonial activities are linked to land or water, and people have rights and responsibilities based on their connections to the country. The presence of natural resources provided an opportunity for people to be together so they could perform rituals and cultural ceremonies and to keep their spiritual relationships with the country (Muir 1998). The Indigenous view is, 'trees and animals they're like our brothers and sisters; we got to care for them; they are part of us too' (Colin Lawrence, Kowanyama).

From an ecological perspective, the feeling of 'oneness' and 'relatedness' to land among the Indigenous people helps them to follow practices that sustain land and water resources. This seems to be the main reason that Indigenous communities have not exploited the resources, but instead have integrated themselves with nature to co-exist as one entity. The Australian Indigenous communities provide a very good example for the rest of the world on how to survive, particularly on a dry continent, while managing their scarce resources and adapting their needs according to the availability of resources.

The Indigenous worldview of 'oneness' nurtures the sense of harmony with nature. It is something we are missing in the present economic world where our focus remains on utilitarianism, consumerism and using nature to produce more and more items to enhance our living. We look at various aspects of our life, such as the social or economic aspects, in isolation of connections between them or with nature.

Edward (1988) presented a summarised view of Indigenous Australians and non-Indigenous values (Table 1.2), which suggested that Indigenous people perform activities for subsistence such as hunting and gathering for food and medicines, as well as for various spiritual and cultural ceremonies in relation to the landscape. Indigenous Australians manage land not only for production gains, but also for cultural, recreational and spiritual values.

However, compared to Indigenous Australians' values, most people from non-Indigenous backgrounds believe in values that typically lead to land ownership or to the exploitation of land or other natural resources to maximise personal benefits. This arises mainly out of greed or to fulfill aspirations for life's comforts that are too great. Our desire to live a 'well off' and comfortable life in material ways keeps us on the run like a 'mad cow' without giving us a chance to realise our connections with Mother Nature.

Table 1.2. Indigenous Australians and non-Indigenous values in relation to natural resources (Source: Edward 1988).

	Indigenous	Non-Indigenous
Natural resources:		
Land	Related, Sacred	Ownership, Secular
Environment	Adapt to	Exploit
Other social values:		
Society	Unified	Diverse
Relationships	Extensive	Limited
Basic Unit	Society	Individual
Reality	Spiritual	Material
Possessions	Share, Use	Acquisitive, Accumulate

How can we develop an understanding of 'oneness' that can connect us to Mother Nature?

There has been extensive scientific research on the status of natural resources, degradation of agricultural and natural systems, and on climate change, sometimes with its economic implications for production systems such as grazing or cropping. However, for the general public that kind of high-level research has little relevance. This book intends to close that gap between the general public and the scientific world by promoting a simple understanding of natural science and linking that to our daily lives. My intention is to promote an understanding of scientific research and to develop and promote new integrated ways to live in harmony with nature. I am aiming to achieve this goal by awakening our 'realisation' potential and by exploring our 'inner world' that will provide us with many benefits.

As a human, we all understand our dependence on natural resources, but most of us do not 'realise' that dependence. We need to instill a component of 'realisation' for our dependence on natural resources. We are a part of the greater system and will face the consequences if we do something wrong. Once we realise our dependence on Mother Nature, then the efforts to save our natural resources will come from inside, and we can mend our actions and develop that feeling of 'oneness'.

The main elements for realising our connections with nature are self-realisation, formal and informal education and the application of holistic perspectives (ecological, social and economic) to life. However, this realisation depends on what we learn and how we learn. In the past, people learned from their experiences and by sharing knowledge with family members while working closely with nature for their livelihoods. So there was a component of 'realisation' embedded in their day-to-day living and in their actions.

These days, we depend a lot on formal education in schools and universities for our learning. We miss informal education for our younger generations. Often younger people do not have the opportunity to talk and learn basic perspectives of life from their parents or grandparents. Some very important perspectives are untouched in formal education, such as learning about ourselves, how to explore ourselves, our inner world rather than the outer world, how to sustain ourselves with limited resources, how to adapt to the availability/unavailability of resources or when to set the limit of having enough. Unfortunately, many parents do not realise that their children need to learn some basic life skills and qualities from home too.

Education to promote living in harmony with nature and for sustainable future development

Education (both formal and informal) is critical if people are to be motivated to take the necessary actions to mend the damage already incurred, and to avoid further damage to the Earth's natural systems. The focus of most environmental education so far has been on teaching respect for nature. In many environmental talks to school children, the lesson is usually to respect wildlife and plants. Generally, the focus on animals, plants or on nature is from the outside, not from an inside perspective to incorporate the students' connections to nature or its components. However, our current education system makes many of us aware of environmental values, but we significantly lack in applying our knowledge to explore our connections with nature, and thus there is little benefit, if any, mainly because of this missing link of a personal attachment to nature.

Ecosystems are the natural systems where all the living organisms interact with themselves as well as with other non-living components of nature, such as land and water. These are fine manifestations of nature to learn how various organisms live in a balanced state. Often the various environmental aspects are taught in isolation, producing a narrow perspective. In reality, the environment's various components such as flora and fauna interact intricately and co-exist, and often we miss learning about this intricate network.

Environmental education usually focuses on certain 'defined' environmental aspects, for example on a particular animal, such as the koala. But a koala can't survive by itself and needs particular eucalyptus leaves to eat and a habitat to live in. We miss the surroundings while focusing on one component of nature — instead we need to teach a holistic view.

Our teachings on respect for nature or wildlife alone have clearly not changed society's destructive behaviour. Respect and appreciation are the first steps toward developing environmentally-aware citizens. At present, there is generally awareness among the Australian public, including children, about the environment but there is a missing link or gap between our own living and the natural environment that surrounds us and supports our living. We greatly lack in application of our knowledge. This is also true for many other places in the developed world. Effective and authentic learning that includes embedding environmental values in daily life should help manifest changes in values and the behaviour of people.

Need for authentic learning

This book highlights some connections with nature that we often overlook, and it suggests how we can live a sustainable way. I want to suggest to the readers not to just appreciate or respect nature, but to also act and realise that our survival is dependent upon nature, particularly in this changing climate. Most importantly, we do not have any other place to inhabit (yet) if we destroy Earth, which we have been doing to a great extent for the last 50 years or so.

There is a need to include some practical aspects of living with nature in our day-to-day learning and in our school curriculum. In the past, children learned to cultivate plants or raise animals at home, particularly in rural areas, and they therefore understood the links between what they ate and what was produced. This experience also provided them with a life skill and a feeling of self-reliance. However, now, with most people living in the urban environment, we need to develop programs that help explain the link between basic food items and our natural environment. This will help children realise their dependence on nature, help them to refresh their approaches at home and develop their own ways to live in harmony with nature. It is of paramount importance for the younger generations to instill 'nature' related values so that they can continue to relate nature to their daily life as adults.

Education on linking ourselves with nature is equally important for all demographics and age groups in our society, and this book attempts to convey the main message of 'living in communion with nature', not in isolation from nature. It aims to change our thinking to a holistic perspective of 'oneness' with nature.

I attempt to achieve the main goal of 'realising' our dependence on nature by connecting our ecological, social and economic worlds from a holistic perspective for our sustainable living. Usually, we look at these three worlds in isolation from each other, which is the main reason we miss the connections between these worlds in our lives. Viewing our socio-economic-ecological living as 'one system' will certainly provide us with an integrated understanding of the modern world. The ecological world that provides us with all the vital basic resources is well-linked to our social and economic worlds. It is fundamental to our living. We will not have our economic or social world if we have no natural world. A social world helps us to live a worldly life in connection with others in the society, and an economic world helps us to make choices to afford the comforts of living. Let's examine these one-by-one in the chapters that follow. Later, we'll explore the connections between these three worlds and the efforts we can all apply at a household level to contribute towards sustainable living. At the end of this book, we will explore the benefits of such a system from a socio-economic, spiritual and ecological perspective while exploring our 'inner world'.

2

Ecological world: Natural environment, modified ecosystems and changing climate

'The trees are like our mother and father, they feed us, nourish us, and provide us with everything.'

— This is a saying in Buddhism (a similar phrase is also common among many other religions and belief systems of Indigenous communities).

The ecological world and use of natural resources

Our surroundings play a significant role in our daily living. Often, we do not realise the value of our natural surroundings, and we take them for granted. Think about a place where there is only buildings and no greenery. Imagine how the brick and concrete structures look without any trees, flowers or gardens around them. We need some natural surroundings that include trees, bushes, grass, soil and scenery to provide an attractive landscape. However, quite often we ignore the value of these precious surroundings.

Natural systems are the systems of nature that support life on earth such as a rainforest or wetland ecosystem. The word 'ecosystem' from scientific perspective is made up of two parts, 'eco' meaning 'house', and 'system' as it's a house system where various living and non-living organisms interact with each other. Our natural systems provide us with many services, goods and benefits. A service or benefit that humans derive from an ecosystem is called an 'ecosystem service', which can be either monetary or non-monetary. The monetary services are items or services such as timber, which has a price value, but many ecosystem services that we obtain from nature are non-monetary, such as clean air to breathe or the aesthetic beauty of our natural surroundings to enjoy. Humans tend to monetise (put a money value on) these services as they became limited or scarce. In the modern times, due to development pressure, climate change and human needs, many of the nature's services are becoming scarce. A very good example is water which was plentiful in the past until 50 years ago, and now has a limited supply at many places throughout the world.

Nature's services are vital to our living. The various services/benefits that enhance our biological (health) and socio-economic living, or more broadly, our wellbeing are directly or indirectly derived from nature. We value nature's services in different ways depending upon their monetary/non-monetary importance. For example, we highly value the monetary service of agricultural production where pollination by bees and other insects plays a significant role. But, we do not usually have a monetary value for pollination. Often we overlook such services or take them for granted in our socio-economic worlds. We'll discuss some of these services in this chapter and how they play a role in our wellbeing. For those services where monetary value can be measured, such as mining, agricultural outputs or eco-tourism, we incorporate their value in our policy decision making. But, for the non-monetary/intangible services (such as pollination, nature' aesthetic beauty or diversity of plants and animals), their role in current policy decision-making is very limited. These intangible services are actually the priceless services for our wellbeing (Fig. 2.1).

Indeed, the various components of our living such as work, culture, health etc., are well-linked to nature. The natural systems are the backbone of our living without which we can't survive.

Our wellbeing (i.e. being satisfied or being happy and being able to lead the life that we want) is directly and indirectly related to nature's services. However, the irony is that in the modern world, various social and economic systems are considered without incorporating nature's role. For example, the socio-economic attributes of human wellbeing such as income, work, housing, health, culture, etc. are mostly viewed as isolated economic systems that contribute to a manmade economy. Moreover, there is also a tendency within us to own and exploit resources to maximise our personal benefits, even though it may cost our future generations.

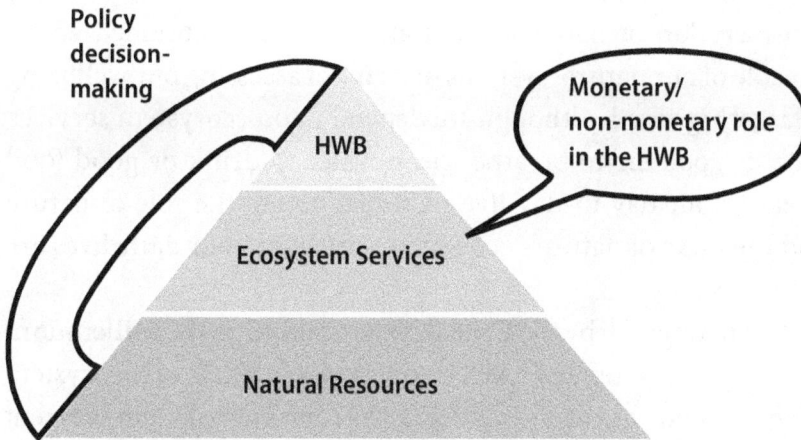

Fig. 2.1:   Natural resources, ecosystem services and human wellbeing (HWB).

There has been a lot of scientific research on the value of ecosystem services in the past few years, with an attempt to understand their importance and to incorporate them into policy decision-making. However, often the policy decision-makers find it difficult to understand the processes and functions of an ecosystem that deliver an ecosystem service. The result is that many ecosystem services are still largely missing consideration in many of our development related policy decisions.

An important field where we can explore the importance or value of natural systems in terms of various ecosystem services is our own wellbeing, as shown in Fig. 2.2. Our wellbeing is mostly related to tangible (monetary) as well as intangible (non-monetary) benefits. For example, we may like to have a good house in a peaceful area where we have access to parkland. We may value that 'good house' for its open space with trees, bushes and garden. From philosophical perspectives, we value intangible aspects of our wellbeing equally or even a bit more highly, especially when we have access to good income or work opportunities.

However, the current government institutions mainly focus on socio-economic attributes such as income, without any consideration of nature-related attributes, as mentioned above. The role of our natural systems in terms of assessing our wellbeing is largely ignored, although we depend upon ecosystem services, such as good air to breathe, clean water to drink or good food to eat in our day-to-day lives. Unfortunately, the role of nature and the links of nature's ecosystem services to our daily lives are often missing.

Recent research by the United Nations through the Millennium Ecosystem Assessment (MA) Programme (2003) on ecosystem services and human wellbeing has promoted our current understanding on connections between the wellbeing of people and natural ecosystems. This research is the first to suggest links between the natural systems and the wellbeing of people. It also provides a framework that includes five main categories of ecosystem services and their links to human wellbeing such as good health, basic needs (food, clothes and shelter) and social relations (Fig. 2.2).

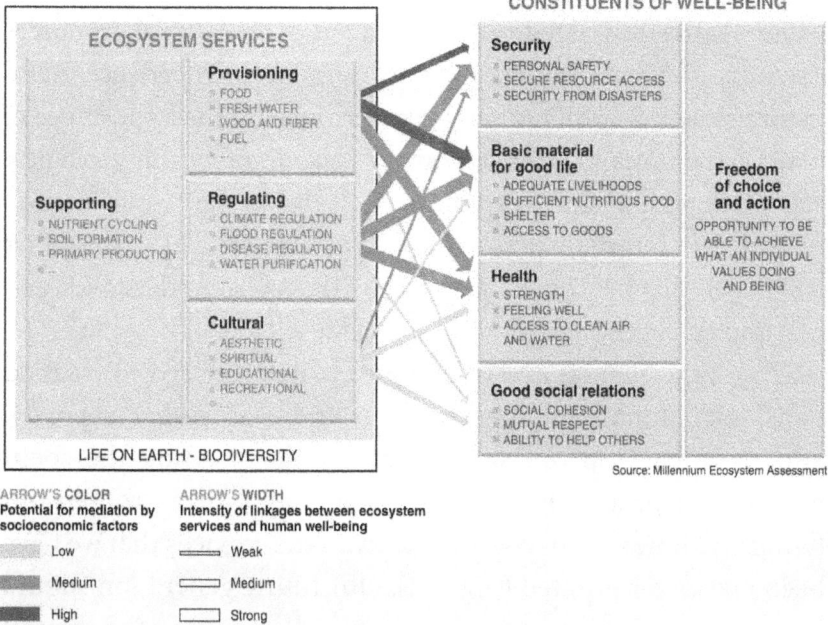

Fig. 2.2:   *Links between human wellbeing and ecosystem services (MA 2003).*

There have been several large regional case studies since 2003 that have found links between various components of wellbeing and natural resources. The primary examples are from European countries such as the United Kingdom, Spain, Germany and a few others where 'ecosystem assessments' are conducted in detail. In Australia, we have not conducted any such large-scale assessment so far. However, the findings are mostly science-oriented and will take time to reach the public.

Many of these assessment studies fail to examine these links on a local scale, where it could provide in-depth knowledge on how our wellbeing is connected to nature. The proposed framework could be very useful to apply at a local or individual scale to examine how one's wellbeing is linked to nature. I think it is important to explore and examine these links in our own personal lives, as we often take our natural surroundings for granted. Examining the links between ecosystem services and wellbeing in a person's daily life will help us to realise our day-to-day dependence on natural resources. Assessing, understanding and realising our dependence upon natural resources will not only help us to realise the importance of natural resources in our lives, but will also improve our ecological, economic and spiritual experiences. Realising the role of natural resources in our daily personal lives is the main goal of this book. It is hoped that by the end of this book the reader understands and will implement the change that is much needed.

Given, the current rate of climate change (Intergovernmental Panel on Climate Change, IPCC (2014 and earlier reports)), and its impact on our day-to-day living including the socio-economic aspects, we need to be aware of nature's role in our living and how we can continue to avail the services that we have been taking for granted (Fig. 2.3). Our future generation should have at least the same privilege to enjoy the nature as we have. I believe that all our individual actions to realise our dependence on nature while effectively using the resources could help us to lead a sustainable living.

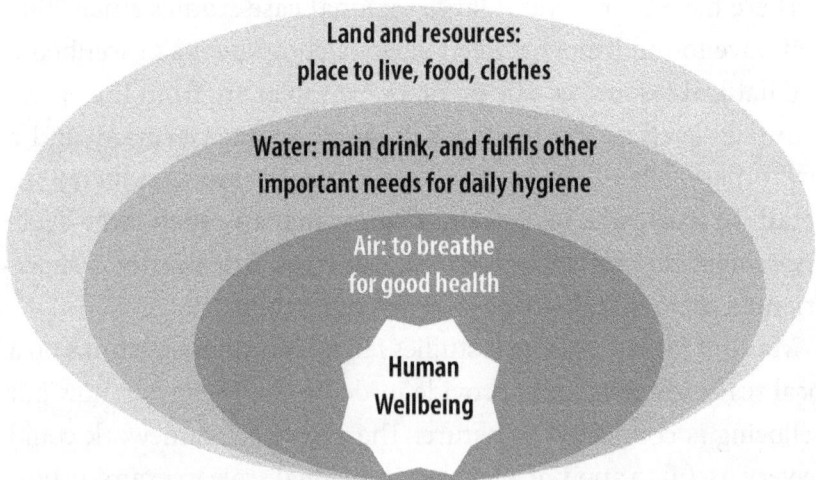

Land and resources:
place to live, food, clothes

Water: main drink, and fulfils other
important needs for daily hygiene

Air: to breathe
for good health

Human
Wellbeing

Fig. 2.3:   Dependence of human wellbeing on natural resources
for our primary needs.

Example

To highlight the use of various natural resources in daily living, I provide my own example below, and you can do the same by answering the questions in the questionnaire in Appendix 1.

I start my day using water as my first drink, followed by a cup of tea with milk (water, tea leaves and milk, using natural gas to cook). Then I eat bread, milk and fruit, etc. for breakfast. I use water for body cleansing. Water is so necessary that it seems impossible to do certain things or activities without it. For example, it would not be possible to have a bath or visit the toilet without water. Then, I use water to prepare food for lunch and dinner (mainly vegetarian).

Natural surroundings (my backyard, as well as a nearby park) give me a peace of mind and solitude that I continue to enjoy for the day. I go out for a morning walk to the park where I like to sit under the big trees and perform my yoga. I get aesthetic, spiritual, and health benefits by visiting this park. This has indeed many indirect benefits for my present and future times. Moreover, I depend upon the trees and other vegetation for good air to breathe, without which I would not be able to survive.

I also go out in the backyard to work in the garden and to meditate for my peace of mind. I regularly take my children to play in our nearby park where they get the opportunity to run around and play with other children. My children help me in gardening (sowing, watering and weeding), learning some skills they may not be able to learn anywhere else. The value of the natural surroundings in my life are beyond comparison and irreplaceable.

This snapshot of my relationship with nature helps me to appreciate that everything I use (directly or indirectly) in my daily life is well derived from or connected with, my natural surroundings: food and clothes come from plants or animals, my drinks come mainly from nature's resources, and the physical and spiritual strength of my body mostly comes from doing exercise, walking and yoga in natural surroundings. I do need a roof over my head, as most of us do, but the materials for that comfort also partly come from soil/rock. I acknowledge that not all building materials come from nature as many are the creation of man. My main basic needs for water, air, food and clothes are directly fulfilled by plants and, most importantly, these services and goods are critical for my living, and these are irreplaceable. This irreplaceability of our basic needs — water, air and food — that we cannot fulfill from any other resources other than nature is an important reality that we need to realise.

I admit that there are often significant human and technological contributions in processing natural materials to make the final product available for human use (consumptive or non-consumptive). The production and processing of food using agricultural advances is a good example.

Agricultural or agro-ecosystems are the major systems for meeting our needs that are often taken for granted or are not valued in a real sense. By 'real' sense, I mean we are not conscious of the importance of food in our day-to-day lives, particularly in the Western world where it is easily accessible and available. We do not comprehend how it would be if there was no food on our plate to eat. The evidence is the amount of food that is wasted every day at commercial places, and even at the household level. We really do need to instill some sense of food scarcity to value this paramount service!

I do certain activities over a year, such as planting herbs, vegetables and trees, etc. in my backyard as well as in the community places; however, these activities do not match my actual use of natural resources, which is much greater. As well as practising, I also intend to teach students to realise the importance of our natural resources to further my contribution to Mother Nature.

Self-realisation

The exercise mentioned above was an eye-opener for me, as I did not realise the full extent of my dependence on natural resources until I wrote it down. To a large extent, my wellbeing is directly related to the use of resources from our natural and semi-natural systems and I, like many of us, hardly realise that in my everyday life. The main reason is that I, like most of us, buy food from the supermarket, store it in the cupboard or fridge and then I use it when I am in need of it. I do not get the opportunity to realise where and how the various items that I use for my living are produced and processed.

This detachment from raw resources is the main reason that we do not appreciate our dependence on natural resources in this modern era. I realise this only when I pick herbs or vegetables from my own kitchen garden. If I was a farmer, I might appreciate this much more. I wonder with the younger generations (Generations Y and Z) if this will be a major problem for many of them. For these Y and Z generations, it may be a major challenge to recognise the natural resources that they are using in their daily lives, particularly when they have not seen the raw resources. In the future, it is possible that only a few would have seen the three main cereals grown in the field that are used by 90 per cent of the human population: wheat, rice and maize.

Realising where our food comes from is a first step towards learning about nature, especially if we want to understand the role of nature in our living and in our socio-economic systems. Agricultural systems are good examples that provide us with various socio-economic and ecological benefits. A farmer is usually better aware of climate changes than a person living in an urban environment. A farmer is connected to the natural resources through his or her production systems and is probably more aware of climate change than the average urbanite, depending upon the distance from the service provided (Fig. 2.4). Changes in climate directly impact on a farm's production potential, and hence on his or her earnings. Direct connections with nature help him or her to understand the role of nature or agro-ecosystems in his or her day-to-day living.

An understanding of our dependence on natural resources will not only help us realise their importance but also how our living is not possible without the support of our natural and agro-systems. This will help us to address many environment related issues, such as to minimise the use of our current resources and to enhance effective usage. It will greatly help us to understand and to proactively involve in managing climate change as global citizens of our common Mother Earth.

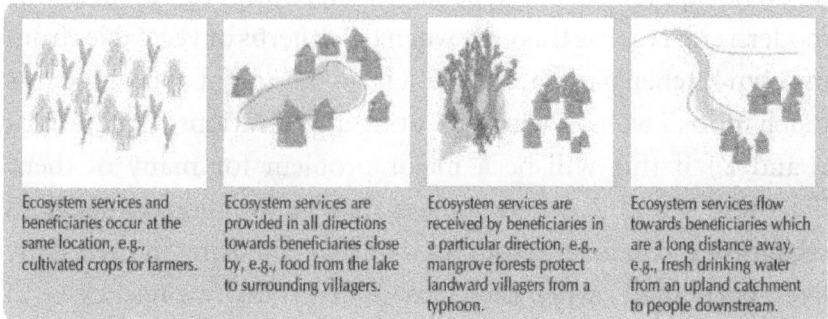

| Ecosystem services and beneficiaries occur at the same location, e.g., cultivated crops for farmers. | Ecosystem services are provided in all directions towards beneficiaries close by, e.g., food from the lake to surrounding villagers. | Ecosystem services are received by beneficiaries in a particular direction, e.g., mangrove forests protect landward villagers from a typhoon. | Ecosystem services flow towards beneficiaries which are a long distance away, e.g., fresh drinking water from an upland catchment to people downstream. |

Fig. 2.4: *Nature's benefits (ecosystem services/goods) at the site of production (e.g. farmers) and for others living in the urban environment (isolation) (adapted from Fisher et al. 2009).*

Global Scale: Use of natural resources

Globally, natural resources have been used at a much faster rate in the last two centuries than ever before. Global forest cover has declined to 31 per cent of total land area. Ten countries have no cover while another 54 countries have less than 10 per cent forest cover (FAO 2010). Global forest cover has disappeared quickly in the past 50–100 years because of demands on nature for modern living. Climate change, increased human use (exploitation) and degradation of natural resources has led to a decrease in soil productivity, food production, air and water quality, and a decline in the availability of other resources that fulfill human needs for good health, housing and recreation. It is predicted that natural calamities caused by changes in weather (cyclones, heavy rains or tornados, or tsunamis) will exacerbate these problems even further in the future (IPCC 2014).

The UN's Millennium Assessment (MA) Programme recently completed the largest assessment of the state of Earth's ecosystems (MA 2005). The main MA findings were:

- Over the past 50 years humans have changed ecosystems more rapidly and extensively than in any comparable period of time in human history, largely to meet rapidly growing demands for food, fresh water, timber, fibre and fuel.
- The ecosystem changes have contributed to substantial net gains in human wellbeing and economic development, but these gains have been achieved at the cost of the degradation of many ecosystem services and the exacerbation of poverty for some groups of people.
- The degradation of ecosystem services could grow significantly worse during the first half of this century, and is a barrier to achieving the Millennium Development Goals (that focus on the provision of good food and health to every person living on Earth).
- The challenge of reversing the degradation of ecosystems while meeting increasing demands for their services can be partially met under some scenarios that the MA has considered, but these involve significant changes in policies, institutions and practices that are not currently underway.

The main message out of these findings is that we have achieved our (material) development at the cost of our natural systems, and we have exceeded the limits of our natural systems; it's time to start mending our ways now to continue to support our living.

Among all the research aspects, the most important aspect was that the MA studies linked the changes in ecosystems to the wellbeing of people and reported the drivers that impacted the ecosystem services on which humans depend for various benefits, as shown in Fig. 2.5 below. These drivers of change are the forces that affect the status and use of natural resources. These drivers impact natural sources both directly and indirectly through socio-economic forces and ecological factors. The main direct drivers include changes in land use, the introduction or removal of species and technology adaptation, and the indirect drivers include demography, economic and socio-political aspects (Fig. 2.5). The impacts of change in climate and pollution are predominantly evident in almost all the ecosystems, including dry land, forest, inland, coastal and marine ecosystems (Fig. 2.6), and the most important concern is that these impacts are rapidly increasing.

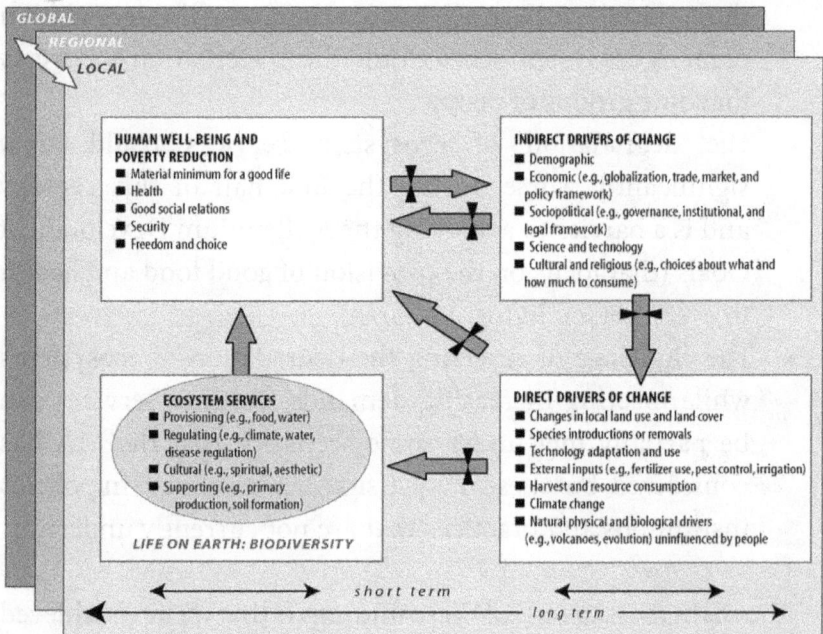

Fig. 2.5:   Drivers of change and human wellbeing (Source: MA 2005).

		Habitat change	Climate change	Invasive species	Over-exploitation	Pollution (nitrogen, phosphorus)
Forest	Boreal	↗	↑	↗	→	↑
	Temperate	↘	↑	↑	→	↑
	Tropical	↑	↑	↑	↗	↑
Dryland	Temperate grassland	↗	↑	→	→	↑
	Mediterranean	↗	↑	↑	→	↑
	Tropical grassland and savanna	↗	↑	↑	→	↑
	Desert	→	↑	→	→	↑
Inland water		↑	↑	↑	→	↑
Coastal		↗	↑	↗	↗	↑
Marine		↑	↑	→	↗	↑
Island		→	↑	→	→	↑
Mountain		→	↑	→	→	↑
Polar		↗	↑	→	↗	↑

Driver's impact on biodiversity over the last century
- Low
- Moderate
- High
- Very high

Driver's current trends
- Decreasing impact ↘
- Continuing impact →
- Increasing impact ↗
- Very rapid increase of the impact ↑

Source: Millennium Ecosystem Assessment

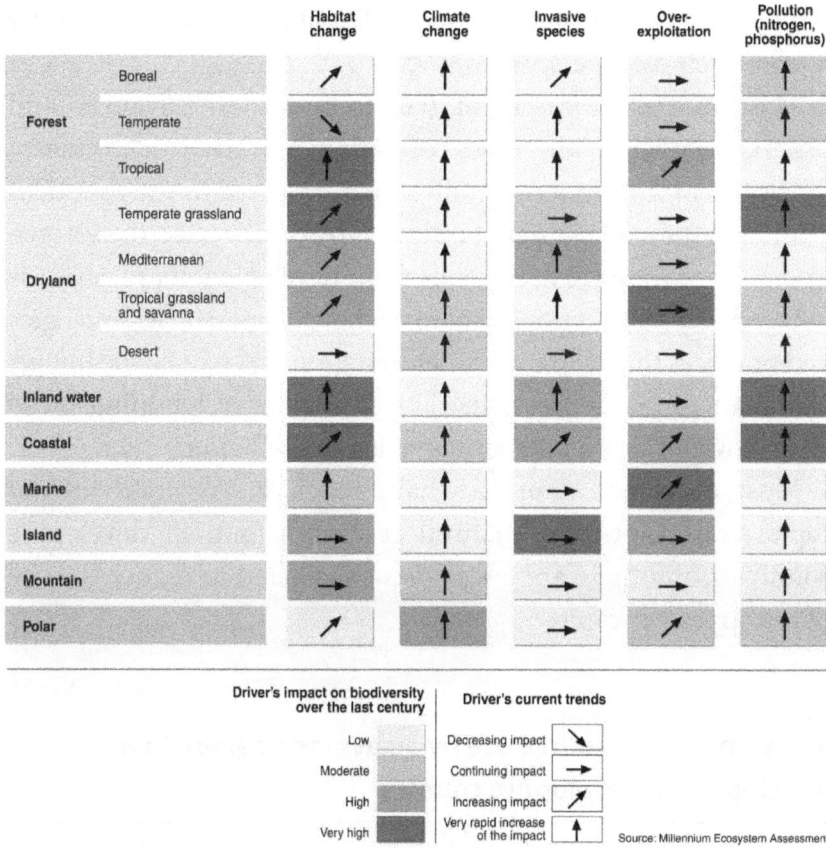

Fig. 2.6:   *MA drivers of change and their impact on various ecosystems (Source: MA 2005).*

At present, the rate of degradation of natural resources is faster in developing countries than in developed countries. Many developing countries want to achieve the same level of development as Western countries, so in a race to achieve 'development' these countries are sacrificing their natural resources.

In this modern world, we are so lost that we do not even understand the meaning of the word 'development'. The word 'development' is most commonly used to reflect material wealth and technological advances. But, in fact, 'development' could be diffe ent to diffe ent people, and diffe ent cultures may consider it from their own perspectives.

Most of the development (i.e. technological advances and material wealth, as the most commonly perceived definition of development) in Western countries has occurred in the twentieth century at the expense of natural resources, either a country's own resources or imported resources from developing countries. It is only recently that developed countries have focused on technologies and practices that help reduce deforestation and reduce the impact of human use of resources, such as recycling waste, retaining forest/green cover or promoting sustainable ways of living.

Most developed countries have much greater rates of per capita consumption of natural resources than in developing countries, and there are few efforts considered to reduce the use of resources per capita.

An example of resource use by an average person in a developed vs. developing country

There are vast differences between the amount of resources used by people living in a developed country and those in developing ones. Of course there will be differences at a regional, local, and even at an individual scale within any developed or developing country. On average, there is much evidence to suggest that people in the developed world use more resources than those living in a developing world. In addition, there are greater levels of green house gas emissions per capita than in a developing country. I can testify this by providing my own example.

I grew up in a small village in India. When I was a child, I used to go to school or friends' places on foot or bicycle. Even when we went to see our relatives, it was either the public bus service or a scooter ride for distances within 20 km of my home. My clothes and food were simple, and I mostly relied on homegrown wheat, rice, vegetables, meat (occasionally) and milk. There was very little plastic waste.

When I started my university education, my use of natural resources for clothes and fuel (petrol) increased, as I was living away from home and visited home every two to three weeks via bus. I think that when I started living in an urban area my use of resources increased, and I became more aware of items that were available for comfort. This may be true, but we cannot conclude that my living in an urban environment was 'developed' compared to that in a rural environment. Actually, I have a strong foundation for valuing the use of available resources since my childhood, and this has helped me to behave like a 'good citizen' (from an environmental perspective) as an adult. When I compare the two situations now, living in a rural environment was much more 'developed' in terms of my resource use and sustainable living.

However, when I came to Australia, my use of resources increased about 5 to 10 fold, mainly for petrol and electricity. Here, even though I am a conservative consumer, I still use a car most of the time to travel short and long distances. I also use more electricity, plastic, clothes and food, as well as other material items of a normal household.

One of the main differences between living here in Australia and in rural India is that most of the resources that I now use are only for private use, meaning I am not sharing much with others. For example, I use a private car and other items at home, just for myself. Whereas, sharing many of the household items would have been a common situation for me if I were living in India, so my resource use would have been much less. Another big difference is the amount of electricity I consume and the amount of plastic I generate as a waste product.

Overall, my use of resources has greatly increased due to my changed lifestyle. The amount of waste I generate has increased from a very minimal amount to large quantities, with a lot of waste associated with the packaging of items I buy from the markets. Another major difference is that I am also a bit detached from the food systems/agro-ecosystems as I am now living in an urban environment compared to my childhood when I was very close to the production system and often I realised the impacts of rain or drought on those systems. Agriculture systems (food, water etc.), nature, and its impacts always concerned me in my childhood, whereas now these do not concern me as intensely as I feel much more isolated from the natural agro-systems!

There is no doubt that the direct use of natural resources per person is greater in the developed world than in the developing world. An average person living in a developed country uses much more resources for living, such as food, fuel, commodities and clothes, etc. than an average person living in a developing country. Many would claim that it is out of necessity, but I believe it's also about the choices we make. We become used to having access to resources and comforts.

I guess it is a human tendency that when one's desire is fulfilled, we develop and go for the next desire, and our list of desires goes on and on. The result is that we put ourselves in a 'mad race' for commodities and resource use. As a result, we put pressure on resources directly and indirectly for our commodities that ultimately result in a lot of waste.

I believe if we attempt to efficiently use our resources for 'good' living, then many more people would be able to live comfortably on this Earth than are living now. Our tendency to collect wealth and materials, directly and indirectly, deprives many other people from access to those resources. The equity in resource use could help all of us to achieve sustainable living. It directly applies to wealth (money) as there are several studies that suggest that if we were to distribute the wealth of the richest 100 people in the world, there would be no poverty. Moreover, this can also solve many problems of environmental degradation and pollution, etc.

In reality, sharing our resources in the modern world is a far away thought as we mostly believe we have earned these and so we deserve them too. As our needs keep on increasing, we tend not to share with other people who may actually be in need. I believe that this kind of thinking, 'to promote sharing', is possibly a little bit unrealistic given the nature of our modern society, geographical and other barriers. The best way to protect the environment is to instead focus on 'realising' our use of resources and to enhance the efficiency of resource use at an individual as well as societal level, so people can live sustainably in the future.

Thereby, I am interested in analysing the current resource use situation — what we eat, waste and/or recycle, and how we make use of the main resources that we need for our living.

Firstly, I will analyse the use of important natural resources for myself to provide an average person's perspective.

Example of daily/monthly/yearly resource use at an individual level

My use of resources:

Before I start, my primary resource for survival is oxygen which is vital for my living. Truly speaking, I don't often realise the use of this precious resource in my day-to-day life to the extent that I am not able to live without it. Certain instances, such as once a lady in a flight was feeling breathless, and she was given oxygen; it made me realise the importance of nature's bountiful resource. Sometimes during yoga I realise the importance of this, but I must admit that I am not doing this in my daily routine. I am trying to inculcate a habit of realising this value during my morning walks and yoga. My use of other main resources is mentioned as below:

1. Daily use:
   Food: 300 g wheat, 100 g rice (occasionally), 500 g vegetables, 100 g dal (mung beans, lentils, chickpeas and others), 50 g sugar, 5–10 g tea, one apple/any other fruit, 5–10 g cheese, some spices and herbs such as ginger, garlic, onion, tomatoes, biscuits, muesli bars etc. I am mainly vegetarian, and often consume eggs and milk.
   Drink: 3–4 L of water, 200–300 ml milk.
   Other use: 50 L of water/day.
   Petrol: 1–2 L per day or 8–10 L/week.
   Electricity and gas: $3–5 per day.

2. Long-term use:

    Clothes: Minimum expenditure (average $20 per month), as I have collected many over the years. Moreover, clothes are reusable and non-perishable items at least for a span of three to five years, given I keep myself physically fit.

    Flying: Occasionally (once a year).

    Housing: A simple three-to-four bedroom house with electricity, gas and running water supply. There is a great use of electricity, fuel (oil and gas) and water, apart from food that directly and indirectly comes from natural resources.

Monthly consumption:

I am usually an average eater, but still when I consider the list of things that I consume per day and calculate my usage per month, it's quite an amount: 7–10 kg of wheat, 1–2 kg of rice, 10–15 kg of vegetables, 2–3 kg of dal, 1.5 kg sugar, 300 g tea, 2–3 kg fruits and other materials such as muesli bars, biscuits, etc. Water amounts to 1620 L per month. Petrol, gas and electricity are the other important resource uses; petrol amounts to an average of 30 L per month; the electricity bills suggest I use electric power worth $70 per month (on average) and the gas bill accounts for $30 per month (mainly for cooking). We also have solar panels that help to partly recover this burden on nature and to offset some of my greenhouse gas emissions that warm up the atmosphere.

Annual consumption:

Yearly this adds up to 120 kg of wheat, 12–24 kg of rice, 120–180 kg of vegetables, 36 kg of dal, 18 kg of sugar, 3.6 kg of tea, 24–36 kg of fruits and other materials. Water usage equals to 19,440 L per year. Petrol accounts for 360 L per year and electricity and gas usage about $1200 per year.

I was a bit surprised to assess and examine how much resources I use in a year, particularly the amount of food that I eat. This is a very conservative estimate for the main items that I consume, bearing in mind there are many unnoticed items occasionally consumed at parties or otherwise. This really makes me think, 'Do I need to eat that much?' It is no wonder that sages and saints eat very little and live longer. I am sure I would be able to survive if I reduce my food intake at least by 30 per cent. Again, it's my habits and desire that make me use more resources than what is required for my living; certainly there is a lot of scope to improve, and I am working on it! I think it will be a win-win situation for me to control my weight while keeping fit and healthy, and for the resources to be used efficiently.

You can do a similar exercise. Please attempt to assess your usage of food resources by filling in the information in Table 2.1 below. You will be surprised (as I was) to know the amount of food eaten over a year. If we add it up for all members of a family over a year, the amount will be much more. If we are careful about what and how much we eat to lead a healthy life, we could benefit ourselves as well as the environment over the long term.

Table 2.1: An account of the food and other main items required for day-to-day living.

Items of daily usage	Daily consumption (amount in grams or litres or numbers) (a)	Monthly consumption (b) (a x 30)	Annual consumption (c) (b x 12)
Food grains or bread			
Vegetables			
Meat/fish/ seafood			
Milk			
Cheese			
Bars, biscuits, cakes, etc.			

Items of daily usage	Daily consumption (amount in grams or litres or numbers) (a)	Monthly consumption (b) (a x 30)	Annual consumption (c) (b x 12)
Petrol			
Electricity			
Water			

Based on the preliminary analysis mentioned above, I tried to calculate my ecological footprint using online software available on the World Wide Fund (WWF) website (Fig. 2.7). An ecological footprint evaluates human demand on nature and compares it to the bio-capacity of Earth. It suggests whether our lifestyle meets our demands on nature within the Earth's bio-capacity or if we need more resources from 'more planets', such as Earth to sustain our lifestyle. Bio-capacity in simple terms represents the capacity of Earth to produce biological materials. In brief, an ecological footprint explains how much a person consumes compared to the amount of resources available for a person to consume. Ecological footprint is expressed as an area of land. For example, more natural resources we consume per head of a population, the more waste we generate and the larger is our footprint.

My ecological footprint is 5.1 gha (global hectare), which means that I need 5.1 gha of biologically productive space to live the way I am currently living. Indirectly, this also suggests that there is a need of 2.8 Earths to support my kind of lifestyle for everyone on this planet. This was an eye-opener for me. While I believed that I was not a big consumer, my ecological footprint suggested otherwise (this worries me a lot now).

The above-mentioned figures on my daily usages of resources and ecological footprint results below suggest to me that I need to reduce my food intake to some extent, though I consider myself a moderate eater that does not consume large quantities of food and drinks. I also prefer to prepare meals at home rather than buying ready-made items. Moreover, I do not go out to the markets to eat and I rarely waste any food, compared to many people in Australia who go out about once a week or a fortnight (at least to eat fast food/take away), and also waste a lot of food. I also think I need to reduce my energy consumption by minimising the use of my car. For the last year, I have been practising driving only when required, without any extra trips. I also need to reduce the amount of waste that I generate, which is not accounted for here.

My Ecological Footprint

Many activities impact our footprint. If everyone lived like me we would need **2.8** Planet Earths to provide enough space.

Here is how my Ecological Footprint breaks down:

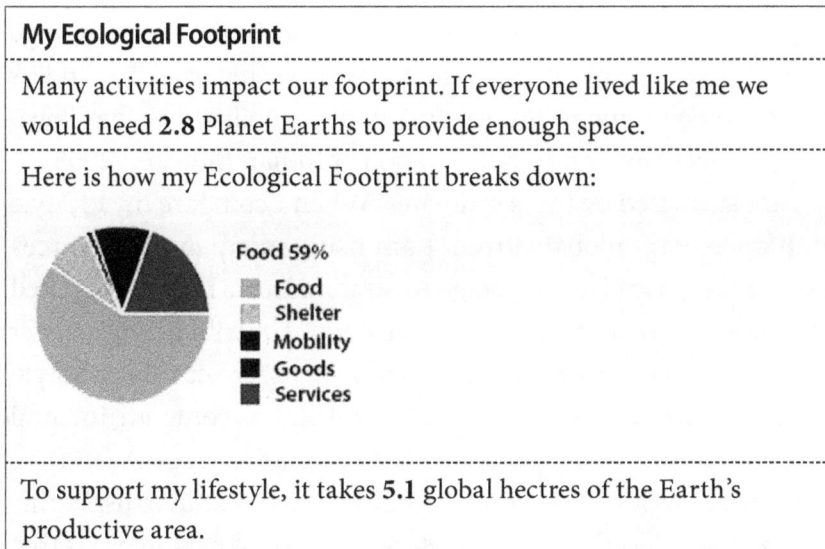

Food 59%
■ Food
▨ Shelter
■ Mobility
■ Goods
■ Services

To support my lifestyle, it takes **5.1** global hectres of the Earth's productive area.

Fig. 2.7:   My ecological footprint results. (Calculated using the Ecological Footprint Calculator at www.wwf.org.au/ footprint/calculator/ and http://footprintnetwork.org/ en/index.php/GFN/page/calculators/).

Note: 1 global hectare (gha) refers to one hectare (approximately the size of a soccer field) of biologically productive space with world-average productivity.

You can easily calculate your ecological footprint with online calculators, such as suggested by the World Wildlife Fund or the Global Footprint Network (at the links suggested at Fig. 2.7.), or using any other appropriate footprint calculator. You should be careful to provide accurate estimates of material usages, living style, wastage and driving, etc. to get the correct results.

Australia's ecological footprint, as suggested in the Living Planet Report 2008, is 7.8 gha per person (the recent *Living Planet* report in 2014 suggested similar values). This is 3.7 times the average global footprint (2.1 gha), and well beyond the level of what the planet can regenerate on an annual basis. An average global citizen has an ecological footprint of about 2.1 gha per year. Compared to this, a highly populated developing country such as India has an average ecological footprint of 0.8 gha in 2008, as reported by '*India's Ecological Footprint: A Business Perspective*', published by the Global Footprint Network and Confederation of Indian Industry (2008).

I am surprised by these estimates. When I compare my lifestyle with an average global citizen, I am using many more resources, whereas compared to an average Australian I am a relatively limited consumer who uses resources sparingly. I attribute my greater than the average world citizen footprint to my current lifestyle, where the use of electricity and petrol has become an integral part of my life. To support the lifestyle of an average Australian person (ecological footprint 7.8 gha) we need 4.28 Earths. Is this sustainable? Certainly not; therefore, we need to explore ways that will reduce our burden of living on Mother Earth.

With such high values for ecological footprints, many of us are in ecological debt. We owe a lot of debt to our Mother Earth for using excessive resources, for capitalising on resources for our purposes, and for not leaving sufficient resources for other living organisms on Earth and for our future generations. As a result, we have initiated climate change, degradation of land and loss of biodiversity at a fast rate in most parts of the world. Our current level of resource use is, no doubt, well beyond the bio-capacity of Earth. One main point I would like to highlight is that it is not possible for us to live sustainably on this planet with our continuous increase in use of natural resources. We would be facing issues such as climate change, food security and loss of biodiversity, etc. much more severely in the near future, which will impact our next generation. It is critical that we realise our dependence on natural resources and, consequently, the value and status of natural resources. We will certainly need to change our ways of life.

Above all this, Mother Nature does not impose any debt on us in monetary terms as our economic and business systems do, despite the fact that many of us damage and/or utilise many things provided by nature. This is a moral responsibility for all of us. Many tribal and traditional societies had such moral values in the past. If we wish to continue to enjoy our living, and care for our present and future generations, we will need to look after our natural resources. We should all know that if we play with nature or nature's processes, we face the consequences too. There are many examples of natural disasters at many places around the world that made ancient civilisations vanish. It is up to us now to realise and mend our ways of living for the sustainable use of resources in the future.

To understand our natural resources from an Australian perspective, let's first examine their current state.

Status of our ecosystems that provide services and benefits

Australian Report (Source: Australian Bureau of Statistics (ABS) 2010 — Australia's environmental issues and trends)

Just a brief introduction to our environment — Australia's biodiversity is unique and globally significant. There are many species of flora and fauna here that are not found anywhere else in the world. Australia is home to many endemic plants and animals and is recognised as one of only 17 'mega-diverse' countries, with ecosystems of great biological significance.

This group of mega-diverse countries covers less than 10 per cent of the global surface but supports more than 70 per cent of the Earth's biological diversity. We are fortunate to experience this rich biodiversity in Australia, especially in the tropical rainforests in the north and the Great Barrier Reef on the eastern coast, both of which provide a very unique combination of flora and fauna and are listed as World Heritage sites by the UNESCO (Wet Tropics World Heritage Area and the Great Barrier Reef). There are 15 'Hot Spots' for biodiversity at a national scale, as shown in Fig. 2.8.

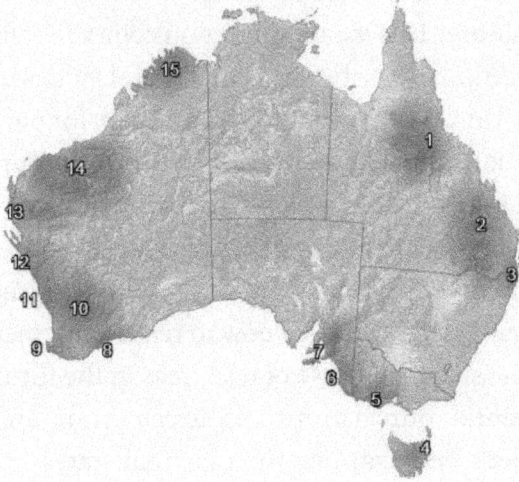

Fig. 2.8: Australia's national biodiversity hotspots (Department of the Environment, Australia).

1. Einasleigh and Desert Uplands (Queensland)
2. Brigalow North and South (Queensland and New South Wales)
3. Border Ranges North and South (Queensland and New South Wales)
4. Midlands of Tasmania
5. Victorian Volcanic Plain
6. South Australia's South-East/ Victoria's South-West
7. Mt Lofty/Kangaroo Island (South Australia)
8. Fitzgerald River Ravensthorpe (Western Australia)
9. Busselton Augusta (Western Australia)
10. Central and Eastern Avon Wheatbelt (Western Australia)

11. Mount Lesueur Reserve-South Eneabba Reserve (Western Australia)
12. Geraldton to Shark Bay sand plains (Western Australia)
13. Carnarvon Basin (Western Australia)
14. Hamersley-Pilbara (Western Australia)
15. North Kimberley (Western Australia).

These ecosystems are a major source of attraction for eco-tourism and directly contributed more than AUD 5 billion to the economy in 2006-07 (Outlook Report by the Great Barrier Reef Marine Park Authority 2009), attracting people nationally as well as globally. Oxford Economics (2009) estimated a Total Economic Value of the Great Barrier Reef of AUD 51.4 billion, which includes both tangible and intangible returns. Many regional economies depend on these natural resources. In major tropical cities such as Cairns, there are many eco-tourism-related businesses (tourism operators, accommodation, restaurants, take-away food outlets, gift shops and cultural tour operators, etc.) and people's livelihoods depend upon the returns from such businesses.

There are major threats to the existence of these precious ecosystems, such as human pressure for use of resources, urbanisation, and changes in climate. Climate change is the most threatening driver leading to extinction or vulnerability of flora and fauna, the bleaching of corals, the disappearance of many marine species and an imbalance in the natural composition of species and their related ecological processes and functions. The reef's existence in a 'good/healthy condition' in the future is a major concern for many who depend on and work with the reef.

For terrestrial systems, the clearance of native vegetation and climate change are significant threats to our terrestrial biodiversity, especially to the flora and fauna in the rainforest ecosystems. As the climate warms up, it narrows the range of survival for many species. Other threats to biodiversity include deterioration of soil and water quality, increased prevalence of dry land salinity, and the spread of weeds and feral pests. Without a doubt, all these ecological disturbances will greatly impact our lives over the short, as well as the long, term.

Th *Environment Protection and Biodiversity Conservation Act 1999* (Cwlth) (EPBC Act) classifies threatened species into six categories: extinct, extinct in the wild, critically endangered, endangered, vulnerable and conservation-dependent. Since the EPBC Act's commencement, the number of listed threatened flora has risen by 15 per cent, from 1,147 in 2000 to 1,324 in September 2009. In 2009, there were 24 eucalypt species listed as endangered and 49 listed as vulnerable. Two species of wattle were listed as extinct, three as critically endangered, 29 as endangered and 44 as vulnerable (Table 2.2).

Table 2.2: Threatened fauna and flora in Australia (EPBA, Department of the Environment, Australia).

Status	Fauna	Flora
Extinct:	frogs (4) birds (23) mammals (27) other animals (1)	flora (39)
Critically Endangered:	fish (7) frogs (5) reptiles (7) birds (7) mammals (5) other animals (23)	flora (139)
Endangered:	fish (16) frogs (14) reptiles (17) birds (44) mammals (34) other animals (17)	flora (528)

Status	Fauna	Flora
Vulnerable:	fish (24) frogs (10) reptiles (34) birds (59) mammals (55) other animals (11)	flora (592)
Conservation dependent:	fish (6)	
Total:	Fauna (450)	Flora (1298)

There are many comprehensive reports produced from an ecological perspective highlighting the number of species that may have become extinct or are critically endangered by various scientific organisations, Government departments such as the Department of the Environment, Australia, universities and researchers etc. For example, Table 2.2 suggests that 27 mammal species have become extinct in Australia in the recent past. Currently, we are facing very high rates of extinction (one of the highest rates in the world), and apparently undergoing a third phase of extinction here in Australia.

What does all this mean for a common person? Usually not much, since we live in isolation from the natural world and do not link nature's diversity with our day-to-day living. This is the major reason we usually do not realise the importance of diversity in flora and fauna, or the importance of natural resources in our lives. These reports are so targeted to the scientific audience that there is no consideration as to how the general public could understand this. A major cause of many of our natural resource use related problems is that we 'the public' cannot comprehend such reports. Moreover, these reports lack any links between our natural resources and our wellbeing or livelihoods, thus a major concern for public and policy decision-makers.

A simple explanation is that once a species is threatened and/ or endangered, there is going to be a change in all the associated ecosystem functions and processes in which that particular species would have been involved. This imposes further consequences for other species that exist in that particular ecosystem. In the end, there are disturbances in the ecological processes and functions and the system starts to degrade indicating the change in its status.

For example, if plant species 'A' plays a crucial role in providing food to particular animal 'B' and then that animal could be a source of food for species 'C'. When 'A' becomes endangered (meaning there are not sufficient numbers of individuals of that species), there will be less food available for 'B', and consequently for 'C,' and those two species may suffer from starvation and may have their numbers decline as well. Moreover, species 'A' could also be playing some other ecological functions such as maintaining soil potential, which will also degrade and have consequences for other plant species growing in that ecosystem or 'ecological community'. Similarly, we can relate this to pollinators (e.g. bees) that play a significant role in crop production and horticulture. If bees decline, it will impact crop production and horticulture. Consequentially, there will be less production and we will be affected through a rise in food prices or increased scarcity of food.

There are many such examples in nature where a disturbance to one species disturbs the whole ecosystem. And if such a species is a 'keystone' species (the most important species, which carry prime functions in an ecosystem), then impacts on the ecosystem can be quite severe. In the tropical rainforests of north Queensland, the cassowary (*Casuarius casuarius*) plays a significant role in the seed dispersal and germination of seeds for many large-seeded rainforest plants, such as the *Endiandra* species. Decline in cassowary numbers is a major concern for the ecologists, as this will impact the survival of *Endiandra,* a main tropical rainforest species.

We depend on our natural resources for our survival and wellbeing. As mentioned in the State of Environment Committee Report (SoE 2011), we need to learn to live in agreement with our environment. But, how can we do so? We inhale oxygen every moment but without realising the importance of nature in helping us to keep breathing. One way to do so is by realising our dependence on natural resources in our daily lives. We probably need to do so to the same extent as many of us think about money. We need to bring a change in our thinking. Just as money is important to run our lifestyle, so are natural resources. Most importantly, they are critical for us to live on this planet.

Climate change has many impacts on the existing state of natural resources that will significantly impact human wellbeing. Many of us are already experiencing the impacts of climate change in terms of heat waves, fire outbreaks, or extreme events such as storms and cyclones. The recent report released by the Intergovernmental Panel of Climate Change (IPCC 2014: Synthesis Report) highlights the urgency of time urging people and the governments to enhance sustainable living while cutting the fossil fuel use by 2100. Possibly, it could be relatively easy to achieve if we understood the importance of nature in our living, and if we developed habits to inculcate and apply sustainable practises.

Australian biodiversity is unique and provides many direct and indirect services to humans. However, our country's biodiversity has declined at a fast rate since the European settlement. This is mainly due to many past human pressures that continue to exert pressures today. For example, the introduction of feral animals and weeds, widespread land clearing, the drainage of wetlands, and intensive harvesting of fish stocks will continue to exert pressures on our environment regardless of the present-day environmental policies, which now prohibit or minimise such actions (SoE 2011).

There have been many advances on the national front to control environmental degradation in the past 20 to 30 years. There is no scope for broad-acre land clearing and for the introduction of invasive species, as we now have a tight Bio-security Act. We no longer develop or use water resources as we did in the past, particularly during the start of industrialisation. Water resources are now managed in line with environmental needs. There have been significant improvements in the past 20 years that will continue to contribute to improving environmental health to the wellbeing of Australians.

However, the major threat we presently face is climate change. Climate change is now considered a severe danger and a direct driver of change in the ecosystems, and it is beyond our short-term or local control. Without a doubt, we have contributed to climate change over the past 100 years (anthropogenic factors), and enhanced concentrations of greenhouse gases will be in the atmosphere for the next few decades. Climate change is a prime risk not just to the ecosystem, but it's rather a greater risk to human wellbeing. For the last 5 to 10 years, there has been a lot of emphasis on adaptive measures. And the theme of this book — to live in harmony with nature — also reinforces the idea of living sustainably within the limit of nature's resources that we have. This involves a deep understanding of how we adapt ourselves to prepare for sustainable living, including climate change. Before we do so, we need to understand our dependence on nature, and on man-made systems such as agriculture.

The World Resources report (2000–2001) states: 'Ecosystems feed our souls as well provide places for religious expression, aesthetic enjoyment and recreation. Every year, millions of people make pilgrimages to outdoor holy places, vacation in scenic regions, or simply pause in a park or their gardens to reflect or relax. As the manifestation of nature, ecosystems are the psychological and spiritual backdrop of our lives' (World Resources 2000–2001, pg. 4). And we, as free-riders, keep on using (some of us even exploiting) our resources without much consideration!

We need to learn to value our resources properly. We depend upon nature not just for food, water and clothes but also for our spiritual, religious and recreational wellbeing. And we do not usually pay for the spiritual, emotional, recreational and many other intangible services. Most of these services from natural places, such as parks for play, exercise, walking, wildlife experiences, recreation or swimming are taken for granted. So, we, in essence, are 'free-riders'. In being a 'free-rider' for recreational/spiritual services, good air to breathe and clean water to drink, we generally take nature's services as guaranteed.

There is no national scale study in Australia that suggests the financial benefits ($) of natural services or changes in their value ($) on an annual basis. The Australian Government publishes the SoE report every five years, but without making any connections as to how the changes in biodiversity are linked to people's wellbeing. On the other side, there are many reports informing us daily, weekly, monthly or annually on financial capital, GDP (Gross Domestic Product) and various financial businesses, etc. This is unfortunate that the natural resources that are the prime pillars in supporting our living on this planet are not viewed with similar intention, as it is for financial capitals. Our modern living in isolation from raw resources keeps us at a distance from getting a real chance in our lives to know what is happening to our natural resources, or to our dependence on our natural resources. In a way, this contributes to people's ignorance, and to their realisation of the importance of natural resources in their living.

Thereby, the main question is, how do we realise our dependence on natural resources?

And, the answer is either or both:

i.   By equating our dependence on natural resources to money for living (using various direct and indirect methods to value each and every service) — it is a difficult task and, moreover, money sometimes is not the solution to all problems. Or/and,

ii. By understanding our connections with nature.

I prefer the second path of building our connections with Mother Nature, which I believe, is the sustainable path that will provide an opportunity for developing a long-lasting bond with nature. The first path is applying human psychology to nature by substituting items and services for money, which may not always be good or valid over the long-term.

Firstly, we know many services from nature are free (air, water, recreation and aesthetic beauty, etc.). Measuring their value in monetary currency can't solve the problem of our sustainable living on Earth. Although, it can certainly help many of us learn the value of free services from nature for which we pay very little or nothing. With a monetary approach, the danger is that many people that have the financial capacity may want to buy those services for money, rather than to invest in learning how to generate or sustain those services. The people with the capacity to buy ecosystem services may not actually value those services since money will be the main target in their lives. They may invest less into efforts to realise their dependency on those services and invest more into earning money to pay for the services, and this can ultimately put pressure on natural resources. So, I believe that this monetary approach does not solve the real problem of understanding our 'oneness' or 'closeness' with nature, given that our living critically depends upon nature. Although, I do acknowledge that at many times assigning monetary values to services or goods of the natural resources can help policy decision-making to consider the role of natural systems.

Secondly, many of these services are irreplaceable and we can't regenerate them by any artificial means, so ethically it is good to preserve what we have from Mother Nature for the continuity of various services for our future generations. Moreover, money is a man-made tool that is prominent in our modern world economy, but not in nature's economy. To me, the answer is 'self-realisation' of resource use and value. 'Self-realisation' is a much more appropriate tool that will enhance our wellbeing and help us to lead creative lives, while making us aware of our modern habits of accumulating commodities that are due to our financial ability to afford those commodities or services. Moreover, given that the modern society is well-educated, we assume that learning through realisation could prove effective (as we know that money is not the solution to most of our current problems).

Let's take an example of the main services that we obtain from our natural systems:

Our land and water resources, which include agriculture, dry land, forest and tropical rainforest ecosystems, as well as coastal and marine ecosystems, provide us with many services without which we would not be able to live. This is briefly highlighted below:

1. Agricultural systems: provide food (meat, grains, vegetables and fruits), milk, cotton and wool for clothes.
2. Forest ecosystems (temperate, tropical and dry land ecosystems): provide services such as pollination for crops, soil conservation, water purification, biodiversity to maintain the productive values of various ecosystems (such as agriculture), genetic diversity for the present and future resource use, good air and water for direct human use, educational and recreational values (fishing, hunting etc.), and spiritual and solitude values for the present and future generations.

Table 2.3 below provides a brief outline of various goods and services (both goods and services are included in ecosystem services) that we obtain from various ecosystems (Source: World Resources 2000–2001).

Table 2.3: List of various goods and services from different ecosystems in the world (Source: World Resources 2000–2001) Primary goods and services provided by ecosystems:

Ecosystem	Goods	Services
Agro-ecosystems	Food crops Fiber crops Crop genetic resources	Maintain limited watershed functions (infiltration, flow control, partial soil protection) Provide habitat for birds, pollinators, soil organisms important to agriculture Build soil organic matter Sequester atmospheric carbon Provide employment
Forest Ecosystems	Timber Fuelwood Drinking and irrigation water Fodder Non-timber products (vines, bamboos, leaves, etc.) Food (honey, mushrooms, fruit and other edible plants, and game) Genetic resources	Remove air pollutants, emit oxygen Cycle nutrients Maintain array of watershed functions (infiltration, purification, flow control, soil stabilisation) Maintain biodiversity Sequester atmospheric carbon Moderate weather extremes and impacts Generate soil Provide employment Provide human and wildlife habitat Contribute aesthetic beauty and provide recreation
Freshwater Systems	Drinking and irrigation water Fish Hydroelectricity Genetic resources	Buffer water flow (control timing and volume) Dilute and carry away wastes Cycle nutrients Maintain biodiversity Provide aquatic habitat Provide transportation corridor Provide employment Contribute aesthetic beauty and provide recreation

Ecosystem	Goods	Services
Grassland Ecosystems	Livestock (food, game, hides, fiber) Drinking and irrigation water Genetic resources	Maintain array of watershed functions (infiltration, purification, flow control, soil stabilisation) Cycle nutrients Remove air pollutants, emit oxygen Maintain biodiversity Generate soil Sequester atmospheric carbon Provide human and wildlife habitat Provide employment Contribute aesthetic beauty and provide recreation
Coastal Ecosystems	Fish and shellfish Fishmeal (animal feed) Seaweeds (for food and industrial use) Salt Genetic resources	Moderate storm impacts (mangroves, barrier islands) Provide wildlife (marine and terrestrial) habitat Maintain biodiversity Dilute and treat wastes Provide harbours and transportation routes Provide human and wildlife habitat Provide employment Contribute aesthetic beauty and provide recreation

Moreover, various agro-ecosystems and natural systems are interconnected and also depend upon each other for various services to provide the production benefits, which we need to sustain our lives, as shown below (Fig. 2.9).

Main ES from the rainforests (RF)

Regulating:

- Hydrological balance (water flows)
- Climate regulation (carbon sequestration)
- Erosion control

Cultural:

- Recreation
- Educational
- Aesthetic

Flow of services from rainforests to agricultural systems:

- Control of soil erosion
- Nutrient cycling
- Water quality and hydrological balance (regulation of water flows at a landscape scale)
- Biodiversity for pollination, other benefits
- Biological pest control (by providing habitat)

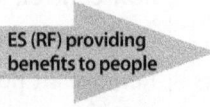

Human wellbeing (HWB)

1. Basic materials for life
   - Food and fibre
2. Good health
   - Good quality air and water
3. Social relations
   - Role of ecosystem services in enhancing social relations such as family relations and support, working with neighbours for crop cultivation, family/friends picnics in the rainforest
4. Security of resources
   - Secure access to resources, e.g. to agricultural land, to the public land (rainforests) and other natural resources
5. Freedom of choice
   - People value being or doing things they like to do (freedom to enjoy various use and non-use values of RF and AE).

ES (RF) providing benefits to people

ES (RF)

ES (AE)

ES (AE)

ES from the agro-ecosystems (AE)

Provisional:

- Food (wheat, beef and milk)
- Fibre (cotton)

Cultural:

- Lifestyle/identity value
- Family (cultural) heritage/tradition
- Educational value

Fig. 2.9:   Various links (and flows) between ecosystem services from the rainforests and agricultural systems for the benefit of mankind.

Apart from these main ecosystems, other natural assets, such as biodiversity are a major source of many tangible and intangible benefits. These values will differ for different people depending upon their understanding and knowledge. For example, a farmer may value some services of biodiversity, such as pollination more highly than someone else, as his production systems may depend on pollination. For a layman, valuing biodiversity would be like valuing stones or rocks, while for a scientist it would be like diamonds that includes many important aspects to support life on Earth:

1. The importance of biodiversity in pollination of many horticultural crops;
2. Maintaining many ecological functions such as soil formation and nutrient cycling;
3. A resource for genetic information for the present and future generations;
4. An educational resource for children for the present, as well as for future generations;
5. Helping to make the whole environmental fabric and integrating the environment's various components into one system;
6. The scenic beauty of diverse flora and fauna, which provides solitude, aesthetic and humanistic values.

Status of world resources on a global scale

World Resources (2000–2001) reported that most ecosystems (agro-ecosystems, coastal and freshwater ecosystems, and forest ecosystems) are facing declining conditions. This is affecting the capacity of these systems to deliver the same amount of goods and services for humans in the future. For example, agricultural systems have affected the quantity and quality of water through the use of chemical fertilisers and pesticides, and this has consequently affected the health and wellbeing of regional rural communities. The report presented a scorecard demonstrating each ecosystem's decline. (Fig. 2.10):

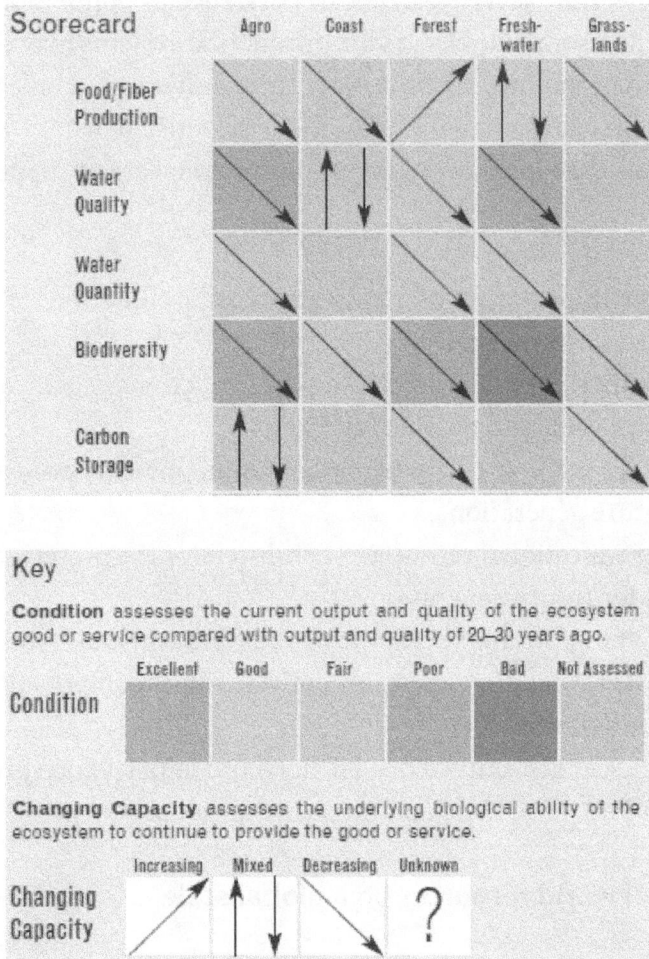

Fig. 2.10: A scorecard to represent the conditions of various ecosystem services worldwide (Source: World Resources 2000–2001).

There are many reports in the developing world where people are suffering from degraded soil and water resources due to excessive use of fertilisers and chemicals. The United Nations Development Program (UNDP) and Millennium Development Goals have recognised and included environmental issues in their future development projects on poverty reduction. There are many examples in the developing countries where people's health and livelihoods are directly related to the environment (UNDP website).

With advances in agriculture, people have exploited the land and water resources and applied excessive amounts of fertilisers and pesticides. This has damaged the agricultural systems, as well as people's health. However, there is not much scientific research that suggests the direct connections between a decline in resource health and people's health. In the state of Punjab, India, where modern agriculture (under the 'Green Revolution' flag) was introduced in the 1960s, people are now facing major health issues, such as cancer, heart problems, low fertility, child abnormalities and arthritis etc., that were not common earlier (Sangha 2014 and Jalota et al. 2006). Due to the focus on the economy, the side effects from the misuse of resources are largely ignored.

While reading about the global status of ecosystems and the provision of services, I am partly comforted to know that the situation is not too bad in Australia, although we are facing one of the fastest rates of extinction of flora and fauna in the world due to previous actions. Generally, environmental concerns are taken care of quickly due to current environmental legislation. Australian agricultural systems face challenges such as soil degradation, overuse of fertilisers, climate change and impacts of broad-acre cultivation (cultivation that largely focuses on one type of crop on a large-scale farm). However, due to strong environmental regulation, there are limits set on the amount of water used from groundwater reservoirs and the amount of pesticides and chemicals used, with minimal tolerance for any activity that harms the environment.

A common perception among the Australian public is that we know about our environment. Yes, we may know it, but only very little. There is a lack of knowledge about the local plants that may be useful for people. Often, people know about the exotic plants, but very little about the native plants. Environmental values are talked about, but not comprehended. It is 'something' that is not deeply ingrained in our conscious. We do not implement our knowledge in our lives. We keep that knowledge or understanding external or in isolation from ourselves. For example, the importance of a small plant which provides nectar for bees to make honey or provides medicinal compounds, is not easily grasped in our lives. The main reason, in my opinion, is that we do not connect ourselves with nature in our day-to-day activities.

Do we think deeply enough about the various benefits that the flowering plants around us provide for their diversity? Think about the number of benefits you can get from a flowering plant in your garden. Sometimes, we do look at one or two of their most important values to us (fruit and scenic beauty, for example) and ignore the others. As nature has its own network, there are many relationships between various kinds of plants and animals, particularly between plants and insects. Nature's network is very complicated and often well balanced, if not disturbed.

We may say that we know where we get our milk, meat, fruits, animals and vegetables. However, my purpose in this book is not to just know but to '*realise*' the importance of those items/ services or resources in our day-to-day life. My aim is to awaken our consciousness for the various aspects of nature that play a role in our wellbeing to such an extent that we realise their value in our mind each day — a kind of ritual to develop communion with nature.

The next question is how can we realise or enhance our realisation of our use of natural resources in our lives? To do so, we need to look at the reasons why we are alienated from nature and its systems at present. Our ancestors, who lived closer to nature, would have never felt alienated from it, as demonstrated by their direct dependence on, and connections with Mother Nature. In a short span of time, particularly for the last 50 years, we have become so alienated from Mother Nature. Our ancestors were farmers, graziers and tribal people that used nature in every aspect of their lives. I imagine we are leaning towards the other end of the spectrum in this modern era, where often we ignore even where our food comes from (Fig. 2.11). I fear that the situation will be worse for future generations growing up with so many modern technological advances, while having little or no contact with nature.

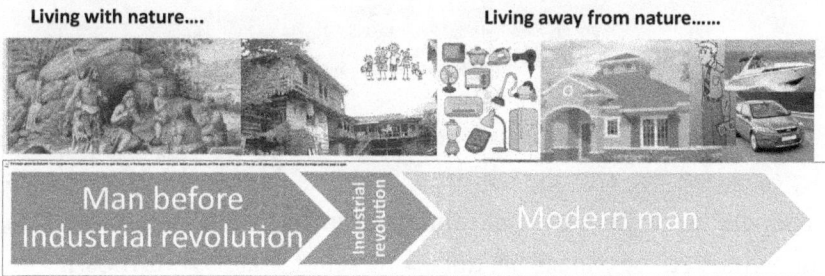

Fig. 2.11. Timeline representing our closeness with nature from our ancestors to the modern era.

Let's discuss the main factors responsible for our alienation from Mother Nature

Urban vs. rural living

Eighty-seven per cent of Australians live in urban areas (SoE 2011). Generally, people living in urban areas tend to have higher levels of consumption than those in rural areas, which is one factor putting pressure on our environmental resources. Whereas, people living in rural areas are generally directly connected with their surrounding agricultural environment in various ways. This could be possible by working in the field, knowing a friend who is a farmer or grazier, or getting produce from local markets. If a local crop experiences a disease outbreak, most people in the region would quickly know. However, in an urban environment people are less aware of food production systems and their problems. If one agricultural company can't access a particular type of product due to local climate conditions, the company may be able to get the same product from a different place. Urban dwellers may not face unavailability of a particular product of their interest, so they tend to remain ignorant of changes happening in the natural environment.

Supermarkets

Supermarkets take into account the local community's dependence on the agricultural systems by stocking products produced elsewhere in Australia or even overseas. In a few places, supermarkets buy local produce and sell it locally, but mostly the agricultural produce travels a great distance before it gets distributed to the local sale centres in towns and cities. The food on our plate may have travelled thousands of kilometres before it gets to us. This increases the costs of production, transportation and labour, as well as the amount of greenhouse gas emissions. Total costs of food production due to centralisation of agricultural produce have increased the cost of food for common people, especially if we consider externalities associated with food production. Moreover, the modern system relies significantly on transportation, which contributes to an increase in greenhouse gas emissions, and hence changes in climate. Purchasing produce from supermarkets also keeps us unaware of where our food comes from, how it is produced, how far it has travelled, and for how long it has been kept frozen.

Large monoculture farms with their 'economies of scale' have a clear economic advantage in the marketplace. In this competitive environment, local farmers and graziers are under pressure to produce enough that's economically viable. Local farmers must also comply with legal obligations. For example, dairy farmers are not allowed to sell their milk directly to the public. The virtual non-existence of local farmers' markets adds to the public's ignorance of their surrounding environment. Moreover, most people have become accustomed to the easy access to food provided by supermarkets. This virtual wall between those who produce food and those who consume it leads to a lack of concern between the two communities. During difficult times, such as floods or fires, this wall can impede sharing of information or can result in a lack of sensitivity towards people in the farming community.

There is now a disconnect between the food
at the supermarket and where it has come from.

School education

The Australian education system does not focus on learning about natural and/or agricultural systems in a significant way. Often, students do not develop an authentic knowledge of natural and agricultural resources that they depend on to live. My little experience in north Queensland with some schools from Townsville to Cairns suggested that there was only one school at Tully that included an agricultural program in student learning, while the other 15–20 schools in the region had nothing to offer on this topic.

In rural towns, agricultural and natural science is only a subject of study if there is a teacher available to teach it otherwise it is ignored. We can imagine the situation in larger cities where children may already have less interest in agro-ecosystems. Agriculture or agro- and natural science programs probably largely remain ignored, at least from a practical learning perspective. Children go on camping trips with their schools to learn survival skills, but how many ever get a chance to visit a farm to learn about the farming systems responsible for the provision of their food and milk?

This is in contrast to the Indigenous Australians' learning system where children traditionally learn about their basic needs such as food, bush medicine, survival skills and knowledge in connection with nature. They learn how to search for food, water and to hunt for animals. They also learn how to look after particular plants, how to use them, and when to use them. The Indigenous people, those who have an attachment to their natural environment, develop a deep understanding of their surroundings. The traditional system of learning paves the pathway for survival in an environment, whereas the modern system largely isolates us and deprives us of such capability, as we take things for granted and want them to exist in our way or for our benefit.

I think there is an opportunity for us to embed a bit of traditional and a bit of modern living so that we learn and relate ourselves to nature while living in a sustainable way.

Our routine lifestyle

Most of us are busy with our day-to-day duties of running a household and meeting our expectations to live a comfortable life. We hardly get any time to reflect on ourselves or to explore our inner being. Working families with young children particularly feel this pressure every day, as they meet their needs, aspirations and raise their children.

As such, our routines do not leave much space and time to reflect or to awaken our consciousness to know exactly what we want in our lives. We run as if in a mad race, and that race goes on until we turn 70-years-old or so when our body starts to indicate, 'It is difficult to run. I must stop before I fall.' By that time, we may realise we have collected too much stuff and probably would have survived with a quarter of our total stuff. It is too late then.

How much stuff do we need?

The generational divide

There is often a divide between the younger and the older generations. Since these two generations now live mostly in isolation from each other, there is less opportunity to learn and share knowledge with each other. I strongly feel that the lack of contact between the young and the old people in families adds a lot of stress and pressure, in addition to the loss of opportunities to support each other. This has contributed significantly to the changes in our social structure and the way we work, manage and run our households.

We also lack a sense of social cohesion with our neighbours, as well as with our elders, and sometimes this is even true of children and their parents. Sometimes parents do not do many collective activities with their children on a routine basis. Grandparents or other elders often miss regular interaction with the family, even if all members are living in the same city.

There is too much 'independence' required by the younger as well as by the older generation. Probably, the younger and older generations feel that mutual dependence imposes responsibility or a loss of freedom. However, when we minimise our responsibilities to keep our freedom, we sacrifice good relationships and lose the sharing of knowledge. We have become a more 'individualistic' society rather than a 'community' based society, which poses many issues for how we can get together to address the environmental problems that require a collective action:

> *The construct of individualism–collectivism expresses the distinction between prevalent cultural orientations that value the importance of an individual versus those that value group harmony. People with individualist values tend to see themselves as independent of others and generally behave according to personal attitudes and preferences,*

whereas people with collectivistic values see themselves as interdependent with others and usually behave according to social norms (Triandis 1995). In individualistic societies, personal goals take precedence over in-group goals, whereas, in collectivist societies, in-group goals take precedence over those of the individual, with personal goals secondary. That is; individualistic societies are 'me'-oriented and collectivist societies are 'we'-oriented (Sivadas et al. 2008).

Our social fabric now exists in 'isolated patches'; the younger generation, children, middle-age and the older generation live without much regular interaction among each other. I would describe our social fabric as very 'patchy'. I mean that the current lifestyle of people who focus on their own methods of living without being willing to adapt to others has contributed to loneliness in society. This has led to an isolation from nature and has indirectly impacted and damaged the natural environment.

The younger generations work hard to be economically better off, and they indirectly put pressure on natural resources to enhance their financial capacity to buy material goods that mostly come from natural resources.

The older generations have collected many items over their lifetimes. Most of those items become useless while some become memorable pieces. We all end up chasing these material goods until we grow old. In this whole life process, we waste a lot of time and energy chasing the items 'needed' for a 'good' life, while we could use some of that 'precious' time to enhance our wellbeing by living in harmony with nature; by doing things that enrich our experience of living with nature and with each other!

I acknowledge that often it is too difficult to live with other people, but we should work out a way to minimise the gap and to enhance the links between the younger and older generations. This may involve giving up on individualistic values while gaining on collectivistic values; it could bring community values that will help to take collective action for sustainable living. It could make it possible to find ways to deal with environmental problems/assets by applying a collectivistic value system. To deal with nature, we do need collective efforts. From nature's perspective we, as a global community, are benefiting and are, therefore, responsible for its welfare. I fear the younger generations are missing out on a collectivistic value system to a large extent!

With our modern lifestyles, many of us often do not get the opportunity or time to work collectively with nature or to grow our own herbs and vegetables. But if we lived cooperatively by sharing responsibilities, we would have more opportunity to do so.

How can we overcome our alienation from nature?

Self-Realisation

Globally, the Millennium Assessment (MA) (a United Nations initiative) findings have highlighted the changes in the ecosystems and their related services, changes in climate, and recently, its impacts on human wellbeing over the past 50 years. A recent assessment by the MA group suggested that there has been a degradation of ecosystem services, which has led to the exacerbation of poverty for some people. The MA report finds that reversing ecosystem degradation is an important target and linking the daily wellbeing of people with natural resources could be one method to prevent and reduce degradation of our natural resources.

Nationally, the State of Environment Report (SoE 2011) says our environment requires national leadership and actions at all government and stakeholder group levels, including the Australian community, to protect it from degradation. There is evidence to suggest that temperatures are increasing and rainfall distribution patterns are changing (SoE 2011). The Climate Commission in Australia produced its first report in 2013/2014 highlighting severe climatic events (bushfires, cyclones and droughts) in the future. Our current generation is largely responsible for contributing towards climate change — a global threat leading to health, social and environmental issues worldwide. We all experience the consequences of our past actions, and now we all should make an effort and contribute to saving our environment for the present and future generations. This will ultimately save the ecosystems and biodiversity for our future generations to enjoy. The question is what can we do at an individual level? And how can we reverse the degradation of ecosystems on which we depend for so many of our needs?

My answer to this question lies in self-realisation, along with scientific research, raising awareness among the public, teaching environmental science in early school education and applying social-environmental pathways. I would like to focus on self-realisation because until we realise how we depend upon these systems we will not be able to care for or protect them.

We need to develop the feeling of caring for our 'house,' as once this house is spoiled, we will not have any other house to live in. So the feeling has to be deep inside us to care for our house — the planet Earth. If we remain in isolation from nature and agro-ecosystems, we will not realise how our sheer existence is dependent on the various services we get from these systems!

How can I realise my dependency on the natural and agricultural ecosystems? The ecological footprint calculator provided me with an idea about how much I consume from our natural systems. As shown earlier, an ecological footprint is a measure of productive land area that one requires to fulfill the needs for living. Calculating my ecological footprint helped me to appreciate how much of my cost of living is absolutely dependent on Mother Nature.

Every day I take away items from Earth's production systems to fulfill my needs, without returning anything substantial (except for educating youngsters and planting some herbs and vegetables). I can say that there are millions of people like me. The issue at this moment is not only utilising the resources, but the 'realisation' of our use and dependency upon Mother Nature for our day-to-day needs. We keep ourselves removed from nature for important direct sources of food and other items that we need primarily for our living, and how much worse this would be for many indirect needs that we fulfill without a little realisation. Our current human attitude completely alienates us from nature.

Alienating ourselves from nature is a cause of many of our problems today, including environmental degradation, socio-cultural and many health issues. We consider the production systems as different from us, which alienates us from the basic necessities we need to survive. We do not embed our agricultural systems into our lifestyle. We grossly miss the importance of agricultural produce, including grains for bread, milk etc., in our lives. Because of our way of thinking — considering agro-ecosystems as business systems — our productive systems have become tainted by a load of chemicals and are largely viewed as systems of economic return.

Similarly, when we visit national parks or other natural places we hardly realise that we, as humans, are part of this whole world that includes 'natural places', too. For example, the air we breathe, water we drink and climate we live in, are all related to nature on a local, regional and global scale. Our thinking has been developed in discrete spheres because of our narrow focus on nature as a separate entity. We, as human beings, consider nature as 'something' humans can exploit but not be a part of it. We think we are the supreme organisms on Earth who have the power to control it, rather than realising we are just another organism on this planet and have a responsibility to look after nature's resources and to share resources with other living organisms.

Alienation from nature, our agriculture systems and other ecosystems that provide us food and other basic items, is a major problem in the modern Western world. Alienation can only be eliminated through self-realisation and developing a sense of connection with nature in our day-to-day lives. For example, using water from the rainwater tank or growing herbs for daily use can help by reminding us of our dependency on nature.

If we see nature with a closer eye and realise our dependence on it for our everyday needs, then we will at least appreciate what nature is doing for us. This may help us to think about what nature is, what services we are getting, what we are contributing to nature (or are able to do) and what we can do to make things better. I'll return to this topic in later chapters.

The 'Sea-Change' or 'Tree-Change'

I have doubts about the recent move among human populations to live closer to nature, especially in countries such as Australia where it is called a 'sea-change' (people moving away from cities to coastal places) or 'tree-change' (people moving to inland/ bush areas). Sub-urban land near the coast or away from the city for inland areas is made available in many cities and towns to develop residential places on acreage blocks. This could have a positive impact on nature if people understood and worked on their land — to grow trees that provide shade and shelter, fruits, vegetables or herbs, or keep animals (if they need), along with reducing the amount of waste by using self-decomposing toilets, reusing green waste to fertilise the vegetables and using rainwater, etc. No doubt, there are opportunities to do something that can contribute towards nature. One could avoid a lot of waste and could recycle green waste on the property for the benefits of other plants. Such 'sea/tree-changers' would be able to reduce their ecological footprint this way. Instead, there are very few 'sea/ tree-changers' like that. For many 'sea/tree-changers', there are usually negative impacts on the environment from such living, as trees are cut to develop an area for housing and there is extra travel for the people who commute to the city from their acreage blocks. If we consider their ecological footprint, I doubt if it's reduced unless people really do something sustainable on their acreage. More of this kind of living is happening in the bigger cities, which is environmentally creating problems in terms of sheer fragmentation of the natural landscape. Scientifically, this type of living also has a huge impact on the wildlife by fragmenting the habitat.

Above all, I believe many people prefer this style of living because of its affordability and a desire to live closer to nature (as a modern style of living), rather than having an urge to do things on their land that contribute to nature or realising their dependence upon nature (which is possible, but still rare). Many people live on these blocks because they can afford and want to enjoy nature. In my opinion, if they are not practising sustainable living and contributing to nature, then they may be actually spoiling that nature. I believe it's mostly for self-benefit to live in the bush rather than to contribute to improving the piece of land.

My rough analysis is that sea/tree-changers increase their ecological footprint. In other words, they put pressure on natural resources, even though they may be living close to nature, because of their choice of lifestyle. The impacts of scattered blocks on wildlife and nature are huge in terms of disturbed natural vegetation, the introduction of exotic garden species, the disturbance of wildlife habitat, the potential impacts of these changes on the surrounding vegetation, and increased human interference in the natural processes and functions.

I feel we, as a society, need to be aware of the environmental impacts, both positive and negative, of living on acreage blocks in the outer suburbs. It would be interesting to calculate the ecological footprints and to conduct ecological, economic analyses for living on large blocks in regional areas as compared to urban living. I wonder if we save or lose (if there are positive or negative impacts on nature) by disperse living.

I think if people living on these blocks knew the land's productivity potential and had some skills, then they could do a lot better! As an example, some of my friends practise an eco-friendly lifestyle in the United States. This is a middle-aged couple. They live on a 2-acre block, which is about a 20-minute drive from the capital city of Vermont, Burlington. They grow their own meat, fruits and vegetables, eggs and milk. They have a barn where there are about 10–12 pigs, 5–7 goats and 10–12 chickens. Goats provide milk that is used for drinking and for making cheese. Pigs and goats provide meat. There is one bull that is used for ploughing, reducing their petrol consumption on the farm nearly to zero. They sell milk, cheese and eggs on a small scale. Apart from this, they use a composting toilet and use rainwater for personal and farm usage. They recycle green waste and generate organic manure on the farm. On this small farm, these two people are quite self-sufficient to meet most of their day-to-day needs. However, one of them still has to work in town two to three times a week. Using cars for travel is their only major energy need. With composting toilets, recycling of organic waste and use of rainwater, there is hardly any waste that goes to the landfi l.

Apart from their own eco-friendly living, they provide the opportunity for teenagers and young adults to come and live on the property in a separate dome house. This arrangement is based on mutual cooperation that whoever stays there will help to look after the animals and the farm, and they all share the food, meat, milk and other produce. In a way, they pass on sustainable living skills to the younger generation. The young people that stay also learn about cooperation and management. In my opinion, living this way is quite sustainable and eco-friendly, and, above all, financially affordable. There are such examples in Australia too. However, I have not heard about a 'green' movement in Australia like the one I experienced in Vermont. In Vermont, young people desire to live on a property to support eco-friendly living. Many urban educated young people actually want to learn and live in eco-friendly ways.

I wish there was a similar movement among the educated community in Australia. People that live on acreage can actually make a sustainable living while enjoying such a property. In the Australian context, there are farming communities that live on a farm growing only one or two types of crops, e.g. a wheat farmer will mainly produce wheat or a cattle grazier will mainly produce beef (but no milk). This is different to the situation I am talking about in Vermont, where a small farm is diverse enough to sustainably meet a family's needs.

In comparison, I would also like to discuss this type of sustainable living from a developing country's perspective. Let's take an example of a farming family in the developing world, such as India where many people depend on natural and agricultural resources for their livelihoods. In many such places, farming communities do live in eco-friendly ways in terms of the farm's diverse production systems where they produce a bit of everything they need for living. Most items produced on the property are used for household needs, and animal waste is used as a resource for fertilisation. A small farming family with only 5 to 10 acres of land can live sustainably by producing their own food grains, vegetables and milk. Although this land size is quite small for an average farm in Australia, it does suggest to us that if there was the opportunity, we could all live in an eco-friendly way!

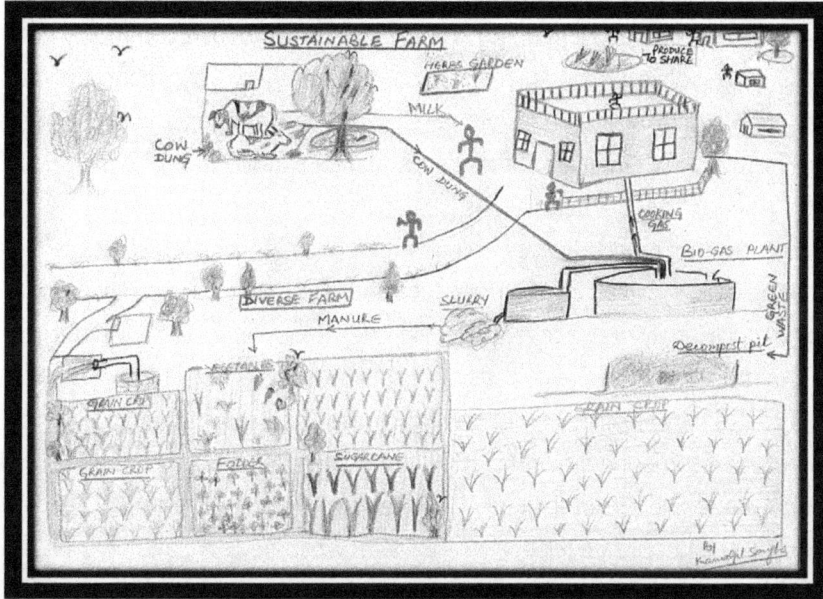

Fig. 2.12. Eco-friendly living in a small village in India.

Eco-friendly living in a village in India

I grew up in a small village in northwest India of about 6,000 people. The wellbeing of the people is connected with nature, particularly with the agricultural landscape. Agriculture is the main occupation and the other important occupations are in public service — mainly the teaching, army and police sectors. There are some well-educated people, but most of the middle and older aged people are educated from grade 10 to 12, while the younger generation is mostly university graduates. The older generation tends to manage most of the farming and related work.

The village economy is mostly based upon agricultural production, which includes producing wheat, rice, maize, sugarcane, mung beans and other legumes, fodder for cattle, buffaloes (to obtain milk, not meat) and some vegetables. An average farmer (5–10 acres) can produce sufficient food grains (wheat and rice) and milk for a family of about 5 to 6 people, and can save some money to fulfill other necessities. However, the amount of money

71

saved is usually a lot less (i.e. about 200,000–400,000 lakh rupees in a year [AUD $4000–12,000]), depending on the crop. This amount is commonly not enough to survive if there are major expenses related to health, education or any other family-related needs. However, if people are in good health and use their resources wisely, it is a sufficient amount for a family to live comfortably given that most of the basic needs are fulfilled by living on the farm.

Security and mental peace become the main satisfaction when wheat, rice and milk — which are the main food source — are produced at a local scale, and a family does not feel insecure, even if they are cut off from the rest of the world in severe climatic circumstances. This is reflected in people's attitude, as they are always willing to share their food and farm produce. Moreover, if someone grows vegetables and fruit, they share the produce with their neighbours or their relatives, and the sense of self-sufficiency still prevails. The people are relatively happy with what they have and they lead creative lives despite their limited resources.

Increasingly in the recent past, due to the younger generation's desires and needs, many families carry out agriculture as a business, mainly to maximise the financial returns from wheat and rice production, and they ignore the role of other minor crops in their daily lives. This is an avoidable outcome of Green Revolution.

Many villages in India provide such examples of 'eco-villages' or 'sustainable villages' where people live on local produce from natural and man-made resources. There is also a kind of social fabric that exists among the various communities at a village level, and people tend to support each other in times of need. These days this is more commonly seen in the mountainous agricultural communities. For example, even in a small village there will be a carpenter, locksmith and other labourers who help the farmers directly and indirectly. There is a level of interdependence between the farmer and other people that live in a village with a farmer sharing the farm produce and others assisting in the farm work. This system was very common in almost all rural areas that were involved in agriculture before modern mechanised agriculture, but it now occurs only in some parts of rural India where traditional (or portions of traditional) agriculture is still practised. These systems are very diverse and are still able to support most of human needs.

This system has led to sustainable living in the past and has enhanced natural and social capital among the rural communities. Many of these parameters are beyond dollar values. Apparently, people may not have all the modern commodities or resources, but they do have natural and social capital.

Unfortunately, this trend is changing in many places now.

Economy of a farming household (5–10 acres of land)

Usually, 4–5 buffaloes, cattle and some calves provide milk for the family, and extra milk is sold for a monthly source of income. Excreta from buffaloes (i.e. dung) is used to produce gas for cooking and to add manure to the fields.

Wheat and rice are used for household consumption and provide the main farming income through commercial sale, apart from some minor crops such as sugarcane, corn, etc.

A small part of the agricultural land is kept for fodder production for every day harvest, apart from dry feed (grains etc.). Usually, this dry seed feed comes from mustard (mustard oil is used for cooking while the dry cake is used as feed for the animals). Agricultural land is mainly used to produce wheat and rice for household use and commercial sale while mung beans, maize, sugarcane and some vegetables are also produced mainly for household use.

On average, a farm of 5–10 acres of size can return 400,000–800,000 lakh rupees (AUD 4,000–16,000) per year, and a family could save about 200,000–400,000 lakh rupees per annum, given a good crop, good health and the family member's working capability. A family usually bears all the other living expenses, such as vegetables, fruits, health or educational expenses for children, and for other household needs (soap, medicine, etc.) through the savings from previous crop production (on a six month basis) and from selling milk on a daily basis. In this situation, if household members are wise, healthy and capable of managing household with their available resources, they can live a comfortable life with modern facilities. If one is content and lives a moderate lifestyle, it's reasonable income to lead a good life.

However, due to the 'Green Revolution' or modernisation of agricultural systems in the 1970s and later, agriculture has become a business with a lot of overexploitation of natural resources such as land and water. Especially, in 1990s and later, farmers have increased their use of fertilisers, insecticides, water and other resources to maximise production, which has led to increases in agricultural cost, and has reduced the margin for benefit. These days, the main emphasis is on financial gains from agricultural systems rather than on finding sustainable ways of producing crops and other products. The result is a chaotic situation in states such as Punjab, India, where farmers exploited agricultural systems for production gains and are now trapped in a web of cultural, social, health and many financial issues (details in a paper published by Sangha 2014). Now, people may have commodities but lack social/community support, cultural values, personal and social wellbeing, and suffer from many health problems.

I would like to convey the idea of holistic living where we, as humans, build and value our social and natural capital as well, not just the financial capital (businesses etc.) that flows in the market.

Living in an urban town in a developing and developed world: a commonality for being distant from nature

The ways of living in urban and rural environments are quite different in the developing world compared to the developed world.

In the developing world, such as in India, the urban environment is mostly overpopulated with people and vehicles, and there is a shortage of natural resources such as water, air, space and natural places for aesthetic beauty. For example, in major populated cities, there may be only a few natural places around the town. There is a lack of good air, water and food — the basic necessities for living. Moreover, there is a lack of space, as people are densely crammed in small houses, particularly in cities like Delhi and Mumbai in India.

In comparison, people in the urban cities of the developed world have access to natural areas such as parks, good air and water. People generally have the opportunity or land available, to do their own gardening in their backyards to produce some herbs and vegetables, depending upon their willingness. Mostly the house sizes are reasonable and provide an opportunity to do kitchen gardening. However, due to busy routines and lack of interest, people mostly do not do that.

A commonality among urban citizens of the world's big cities is that they usually do not contribute to nature. People in the developed world are either too occupied or lack the skills, whereas people in overpopulated developing countries, such as India and China, are not able to do any gardening due to lack of space.

There is a scope for people living in the developed world, that have access to the land/backyard to do something differently, that is, growing fruits, vegetables and herbs in their gardens, getting to know their natural surroundings and to value nature's services in their lives. There is a need for motivation within the urban community, which will help them understand farmers' perspectives and will also provide multiple socio-cultural benefits for the community.

In this chapter, we have discussed the role of natural resources in our living, the status of natural resources, nationally as well as globally, including current environmental issues and the factors that are responsible for our alienation from Mother Nature. We have explored the main factors that contribute to our current disconnect with nature. I acknowledge that there are many other social-economic and cultural reasons for this too. As a global citizen of Mother Earth, it's our responsibility at this crucial time to act in a way that is sustainable, and that contributes positively to nature. In the next chapter, we'll explore how we can connect ourselves with nature.

3

Creating realisation in our daily lives

A human being is a part of the whole called by us the "Universe", a part limited in time and space. He experiences himself, his thoughts and feelings as something separated from the rest, a kind of optical delusion of his consciousness. This delusion is a kind of prison for us, restricting us to our personal desires and to affection for a few persons nearest to us. Our task must be to free ourselves from this prison by widening our circle of compassion to embrace all living creatures and the whole of nature in its beauty.

— Albert Einstein

Realising our connections with nature

Value of our natural surroundings

Do we value our natural surroundings? How much do we appreciate these surroundings? Most of us think of parks and creeks as a place to go for a morning or evening walk, but do we think about the surroundings when we walk there? What do they do for us? What kind of benefits do we get from those systems?

Generally when people go for a walk, they only recognise one or two natural values, such as aesthetic beauty. But we get many benefits from our natural surroundings, such as oxygen to breathe (and to take in the carbon dioxide that we produce), a shelter for birds and other animals, the spiritual sensation and a place for recreation. In our daily lives, we do not usually value these benefits. Here are a few examples and explanations from my perspective:

1. A tree in a roundabout

    I have always admired a single, lean and small tree elegantly standing in the middle of a roundabout, which contributes towards oxygen production while absorbing carbon dioxide and pollution from the many vehicles that pass by. It provides aesthetic beauty to the place. It is a symbol of 'resilience', 'giving' and 'survival' in harsh conditions.

A single tree growing in a round about
and providing multiple benefits.

2. Walking on the beach

    Quite often, I like to walk on the beach, to enjoy the ocean breeze. The view, the vastness and openness, the unique vegetation and fauna, the solitude and the ocean sounds provide many benefits for healthy and spiritual living. Another special benefit of the beach is recreational fishing.

3. Parks and nature conservation areas
    When we visit parks and nature conservation areas, there
    are multiple benefits from a peaceful and clean environment,
    including spiritual, aesthetic, recreational, health and
    educational benefits. Often people enjoy camping because
    it is a chance to spend time in and connect with nature.

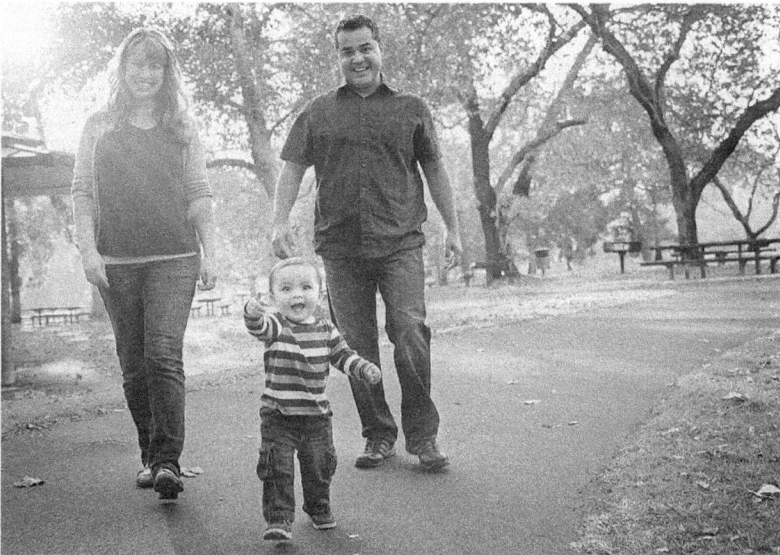

4. Backyards

Many benefits are obtained from just visiting our own backyards to relax and calm our minds. It provides a quiet environment to relax, to work with the soil and to experience a deep spiritual connection with nature. Working with the soil also helps us to meditate, and thus provides healthy and spiritual benefits.

5. Our surroundings in a residential area

Most people prefer that the surroundings of their dwellings are peaceful and beautiful. Often residential areas have an avenue of trees lining the streets, which provides an attractive feature. One can particularly notice this difference when visiting newly developed areas where house structures may be modern and beautiful, but quite often lack natural beauty. I often feel that newly developed areas, without trees or with small trees, are bare and compromise the area's beauty. This is apparent when you compare such an area with older, developed residential areas where trees line the streets and add to the residential buildings beauty. The presence of trees adds to the houses pleasure value.

These are just a few simple examples suggesting that we need to view our surroundings from nature's lens and to recognise these benefits whenever we visit or are in touch with such places.

How do we realise our daily dependence on nature?

We talked about realising our dependence on Mother Nature by valuing the benefits, appreciating our surroundings and doing something with nature, but how can we do so? One simple step would be to make a simple table to look at as an everyday reminder (Table 3.1):

Table 3.1. List of our basic needs

Basic items for human needs	Where we get it from	Raw materials or ultimate source	How much do I use?
Grains/Bread			
Vegetables and fruits			
Meat			

Basic items for human needs	Where we get it from	Raw materials or ultimate source	How much do I use?
Milk			
Water			

This table could be printed and placed in the kitchen for ticking. It could also be an important item on your modern technology devices such as iPhone, iPad or tablet, etc. requiring you to fill-in information every day.

Another idea is to have a picture of a farm from where we obtain most of our basic materials and to hang it in the kitchen. Its purpose is to remind us of our daily dependence on Mother Nature. No matter how much money we earn, we can't survive just on money. Money is a tool to buy the materials we need. Among these materials, our very basic needs include food, and our food comes from the natural and agricultural systems. In the current madness for material goods, we need to constantly reinforce that food, which comes from natural and agricultural systems, is our prime need for survival. This is also the basis for healthy and spiritual wellbeing. We need to continue to develop a sustainable system and its processes over the long term for our coming future generations.

Main resources for which we depend upon nature

Food is one of our basic needs for survival, as discussed in the coming sections. Apart from food, there are many other needs that are fulfilled from natural resources such as water, air, paper, spiritual needs, recreation, etc.

Think about living without water. Think about resources such as paper that we all use around our households so commonly, without realising how much we use or how much we waste! I'll use the following simple examples to provide an overview of resource use in relation to our attitude.

Resource use of paper and water

Let's examine how we use some daily resources, such as paper and water:

1. Paper

Paper is a significant resource we all need in our daily lives, but we often do not value it. Material wealth and the economic capacity (including other factors, such as globalisation) to buy the materials has led to its overproduction, which results in low costs as well as in overconsumption.

How do we use paper? What is our attitude to value this resource?

Most of us use paper, liberally, for writing, printing, and for many other uses. We do not try to conserve paper, and mostly we do not value it as a resource. It is one item that is wasted quite frequently around every household.

Paper is, particularly, used freely by school students. Often in schools there is a general attitude that students just tear apart a page if they write a word incorrectly. There is very little emphasis on correcting spelling or other mistakes using the same page. I was surprised to see this kind of behaviour during my teaching experience in schools (particularly among high school children), and I wondered what the next generation was learning about these resources. How will they value this resource in the future? Often, I just wondered about the student's attitude as they were in a perfect learning environment, but the values instilled in them or what they learned from their teachers and at home did not reflect any positive attitude towards paper — the most necessary resource for learning.

Compared to this, my experience as a child in a developing country helped me to realise the importance of such a resource early on. I valued those resources, as I could not afford to go to the market to buy another notebook. We used paper judiciously, as it was such an important resource for learning. Partly, it involved respect as paper and books are the main media to enhance one's learning (this must be a cultural influence). There was no chance of tearing a page from a notebook.

Actually, this was also true for many other items such as pencils and pens. We made efficient use of pencils and reused pens (with refills) due to the limited availability of these resources. To respect and value resources for learning was, I feel, a positive attitude instilled in me at a young age, and one which I have capitalised on throughout my life.

Some facts about paper:

Paper (depending upon the type and quality) is usually made from soft wood, saw wood or chip wood (that otherwise may go to waste), but trees are also cut (or sometimes re-grown) to provide this wood. Some rough facts are:
- 1 carton (10 reams) of 100 per cent virgin copier paper uses 0.6 trees.
- 100 reams uses 6 trees.
- 1 ream (500 sheets) uses 6 per cent of a tree.
- 1 tree makes 16.67 reams of copy paper, or 8,333 sheets.

In simple words, if we use approximately 8000 sheets in a year, we sacrifice one tree, and in our lifetime, for example 40 years of writing, learning, business and work, we use about 40 trees. This is a conservative figure. But if we think on a national scale for approximately 20 million people in Australia, 8 billion trees are cut down within those 40 years, or, in other words, 20 million trees are cut down per year. It is true that we recycle paper and we use only soft wood trees for paper production grown for this purpose. But the alternative is that trees are trees and they could have been used to fix the excess amount of carbon dioxide and to provide many other benefits for humans if we could use paper judiciously. If we used paper carefully then we would need to cut much less, and leave the others to grow!

It is important to note that our use of paper also involves various items wrapped in paper or hard cardboards, so our actual use will be much more than just 8000 sheets per year.

No doubt recycling of paper helps to save trees, but it also consumes energy and resources that we need to account for as well (Fig. 3.1).

Fig. 3.1. Paper and trees conversion.

Now that paper is a readily and cheaply available resource, we value it less. How can people cultivate the value of a resource that is available at such a low price? Of course, there are many other big things to consider for sustainable living. However, we can start with little ones, which are fundamental to our learning. Our children should be learning to value this basic resource from the very beginning of their schooling.

Similarly, I wonder why we can't refill our ballpoint pens, as every time it runs out it is the ink that runs out, not the ballpoint pen. Still, we have to throw the ballpoint pens away because refills are rare, and it is easier to buy a new one. Although many things could be easily reused, we are not in the habit of reusing them. In the end, it all comes down to the availability of a resource and its affordability. Since almost all of us can easily afford to buy these resources, instead of using them in a judicious way, we get in the habit of using them in a liberal way.

Another aspect of this attitude towards paper and pens is that because we know these materials are recycled, we are more inclined to throw them away. My argument is that recycling itself is an energy-consuming process. Every time we recycle something it does not come to the same level as the initial materials used to produce it, and some materials (and energy of those materials) are always wasted in every recycling process. Given that there are energy use and wastage, there is a need to find ways to educate people to efficiently use and re-use some of these materials.

There is no doubt that recycling saves materials such as wood, and that making paper from used paper uses less energy. The US Environmental Protection Agency estimated that producing a recycled paper product requires only 60 per cent of the energy that is required to create one from fresh wood pulp. Roughly, recycling a ton of paper can save 17 trees. Recycling paper also requires about half the water normally used in processing paper from virgin wood.

How paper is produced and recycled

Paper is produced from wood pulp. Softwood trees are cut for pulp and processed through the paper mill for pulping, cleaning and rolling to finally make the paper rolls. For recycling, there are a few extra steps involved such as collection and transportation, sorting, re-pulping and screening, and de-inking (Fig. 3.2). Approximately 60–80 per cent of the recovered paper is recyclable, and the rest is considered waste and goes to a landfill, mainly due to wires, plastics, staples, etc. Recovered paper can be recycled up to five to six times and then the wood fibres become too brittle to form the paper.

Going back to the main topic of financial capacity to afford items such as paper, it is reasonable that people with the means do not hesitate to use this resource. I hope that if we combine the two efforts, less wastage and reuse, we can sustainably meet our needs. Recycling paper is an energy-efficient process, but we also need to learn and teach the younger generations and ourselves that these resources are precious.

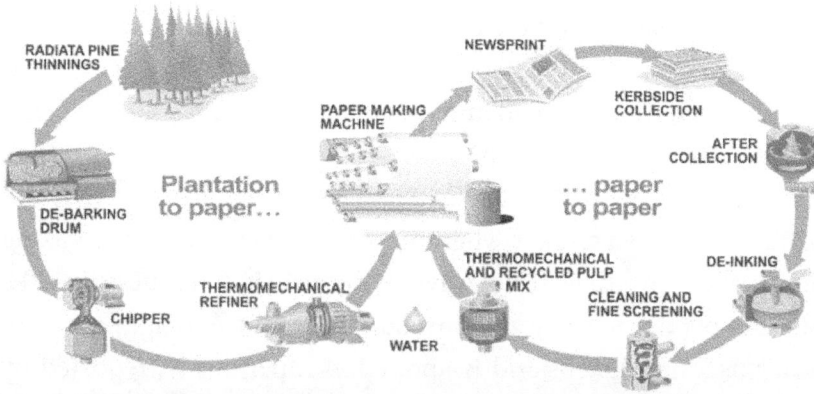

Fig. 3.2.   Paper production (source: Bowen Island Recycling Depot)

2. Water

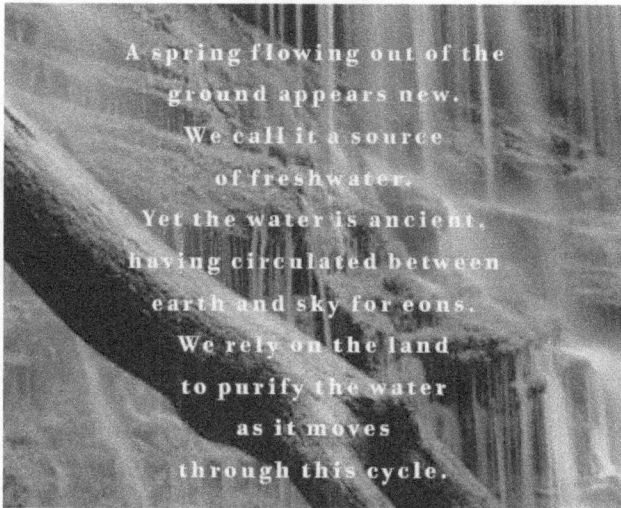

A spring flowing out of the
ground appears new.
We call it a source
of freshwater.
Yet the water is ancient,
having circulated between
earth and sky for eons.
We rely on the land
to purify the water
as it moves
through this cycle.

Fig. 3.3.   From the front page of the World Resources Report 2000–2001: *underlying the links between our most precious resources — water and the land.*

Among our prime needs for living, water is the most precious resource that nature provides (Fig. 3.3). Let's examine its usage and our attitude towards it.

Probably, the first thing we need when we wake up in the morning is water: to drink, to wash or refresh us, or to be used for cleansing/toilet activities. However, because water is frequently available (or made available in many places in the developed world by technological advances), we do not realise we are using this resource and we do not value this resource on a daily basis.

How many people think that when they flush the toilet they are using 3–5 L of water? Or when they take a shower, they are using another 40–60 L of water? An average person uses about 100–200 L of water per day for various household activities. Average per capita water used in Queensland is about 154 L/per day as reported by the Queensland Water Commission. But, we do not realise the value of this resource, and how critical it is in our lives, as there is a reliable supply, and we are accustomed to that service.

Think about what would happen if the taps supplying water to your household ran out one day. The continuous and reliable supply of it has made our lives very comfortable. A reliable supply of water has become a part of our lives, and we usually see this resource as readily available, hot or cold, and without any delay. We have become accustomed to taking this resource for granted. The question is: how much do we realise the importance of water in our lives? And this is further linked to how we use this resource.

Efficient use of water

Water is a basic necessity for living. We cannot live without water. But we overexploit this resource on many occasions. Readily available tap water has made us accustomed to its comforts without realising the amount we consume or how we consume it.

Hand-pumped water is still used in many places in the world

where water is either scarce or it is impossible to secure a regular and reliable water supply to a town for financial reasons. Many people, particularly children, spend their whole day collecting water from a common source such as a hand pump, bore or pond. In the developed world, the water supply is a reliable service in the form of council or municipal tap water and/or bore water on larger properties. Technology has given us easy access, but this has resulted in interference in nature's ways and has led to its overuse and exploitation.

It is important to note that use of water is also linked to climate and geography of a place, including the region's cultural landscape. Within a developing country, you will be able to see different ways of getting water: tap water (municipal supply), personal bore/tap water, hand pumps or collection from a pond — depending on the financial affordability, geography and availability of resources. In financially affluent areas within developing countries such as India where water supply is limited, people are required to pay for their water use, and there can be cuts to the water supply to address a water shortage. As a result, most people feel the significance of this resource in their daily life.

In the developed world, although we mostly recognise that water is a precious resource and is of prime importance for human survival, I question how much we value this resource in our daily lives, thinking in depth about this resource, its value and our attitude toward water. A major concern to me is our current attitude towards the use of this precious life-saving resource where we don't efficiently use this resource rather we let it waste down the drain!

In the olden times, a hand-pump would have saved the amount of water used by people since one has to work hard to pump water out for usage. Doing so helped people realise the value of water, which directly or indirectly resulted in judicious use. However, with today's lifestyle and technological advances, this procedure is not feasible.

In developed countries, where tap water is readily available in most places, our average (minimum) daily usage is approximately 100–200 L per day and at times it can be a lot higher — sometimes even up to 400 L/day/person. We use approximately 60 L of water just for showering.

The major drawback with the current tap water system in developed countries is overuse without actual realisation. A common tendency of our government policy is to meet the public's needs without compromising their comfort. This has led to an attitude towards water usage that is too liberal, and our current habits for overuse of water are the result of such an attitude. Another important aspect is that for people in developed countries even though in some places water is limited, with technological advances there is still a continuous supply. This suggests we have moved away from adapting ourselves to the availability of a resource to a state where we make the resource available to us for our comforts without considering its availability.

There is an urgent need today to realise our daily dependence upon water, but how can we do so? Cuts in the water supply, recycling water or pricing water are the main strategies that would help people realise its value. A lot of emphasis, so far, is put on recycling water or pricing water, rather than doing something to help people 'realise' the use of this resource or to change people's attitudes. Let's look at the possible options that may help us to learn judicious use of water.

One possible way would be to introduce water cuts. An interrupted water supply will help people to think about water and will help them realise the resource value without any additional financial pressure on them.

Recycling water is also a good way, but we can't use recycled water for drinking as people are wary of such a water supply in Australia (however, this is acceptable in many other parts of the world such as Singapore and Israel).

Introducing water pricing is another method, particularly in the agriculture sector or where water is needed in large quantities. Many city councils in Australia, especially in major cities have introduced water charges. However, this is again linked to financial affordability and will not change people's attitude towards this resource over a long-term period. With time, people get used to paying for water charges. I remember when water charges were first introduced in Townsville, Queensland, by the city council (around 2005–2006), there was a big outcry from the public, but with time people became used to paying their water bills. Various city councils have also implemented conservation measures to address water shortage, particularly in drought years. Interestingly, many studies reveal only a temporary change in people's attitude during crisis such as drought events, and that over time people go back to their normal habits. During drought periods, the temporary attitudinal change could be used to realise the importance of this vital resource in our day-to-day life.

I think a combination of these strategies could work to change our attitude towards water usage. Firstly, 'cuts' in the water supply during drought periods is one major step that could help us to realise the value of water as a resource. Secondly, using rainwater is a really good way of saving water for a reliable supply and could be implemented at each household level.

While I partially agree with pricing water, I fully agree with recycling water and the use of rainwater. Pricing water may not bring a change over the long term in our attitude or may only bring a little change in realising our dependence. Scarcity or restricting availability of water may help to change our attitudes, as well as the use of water. In many circumstances, people value the resource once it is scarce. For example, in Toowoomba, Queensland, many people installed rainwater tanks when there was a drought about 10 years back. That drought incident instigated people to value this precious resource and to use water more judiciously. But with time, as the water levels reached normal, people have lost that consciousness and realisation (or it does not exist to the same extent as it did 10 years ago) and are back to their normal water usage levels.

These are normal human attitudes, and one can expect that if we have a resource sufficiently available, then why don't we use it? To me, the main point is that we have set high levels of consumption for this resource from the beginning, and when we had to re-adjust our consumption, it required a 'significant' change. We applied that change by installing rainwater tanks and adapting to conservation water measures. In my opinion, we intended to supplement our supplies without much compromise. Undoubtedly it is good to install rainwater tanks. However, over time, since we did not have a 'significant' change in our attitude, we just went back to our original levels of consumption rather than adjusting ourselves to the reduced use of water. Since our original levels of consumption were already set high, any change or reduction of those levels is considered a significant change. I would like to emphasise that we also need to learn to adjust ourselves to the levels of resource availability and to be adaptable to those levels using supplemented sources (rainwater, recycled water, etc.).

Our attitudes to using a resource and adapting to its availability are of the utmost importance, not just during drought conditions but at other times too.

In summary, there are a few options to help us realise the value of water in our lives:

1. Pricing water, as most city councils do in Australia, is one way, but this is a monetary approach. The council pricing is based upon standard water charges (with set limits for a certain degree of use), rather than the individual household usage (price per ML use of water). Introducing water charges on a per unit basis (as for electricity usage) rather than the standard household rates will help to raise awareness among the public about water usage. However,

as I mentioned above, with financial affordability, people will get used to this, and it may not change their attitude to value water as a resource. This is the most common approach widely applied in many places. However, the long-term effects of such an approach are questionable.

2.   Introducing planned water cuts. This will make the public realise the value of the resource by making it unavailable at certain times. If council water supply is less frequent and interrupted, this will help people to think about this resource. Currently, most of us think that turning the tap on means water is going to flow. We never expect that these taps could be dry one day. However, there would be, of course, political concerns about this strategy.

3.   Introducing unannounced cuts once every six months or yearly. Although it will lead to an outcry from the public, short-term unannounced cuts could help the public realise how important water is in day-to-day living.

4.   General awareness through public meetings, posters and environmental awareness campaigns.

In the end, water is life. We all need to take some actions at a personal level to conserve and efficiently use this resource.

3. Food

Our major issues related to the availability of food in the future

Presently, in Australia, we have enough natural resources to provide us with food, milk, water and other much needed items for living. However, with time and changes in climate, the availability of resources will decline. Production of food in changing climate conditions will be challenging. Food security and the provision of food will become important issues in the future.

Globally, the Food and Agriculture Organisation (FAO

2010a) has predicted an increased demand for food due to the increase in global population, as well as increased impacts on our production systems from climate change that will adversely affect food security. Thus, food prices are expected to soar.

In Australia, many farmers are entering into their early-old age phase. And there are fewer chances, or in other words favourable policies, for the younger generations to live on the farm to make their living. Most children from regional and rural areas usually move to urban cities to seek education, jobs or other work-related opportunities. The younger population in the small towns is slowly being phased out. There are many examples of 'ghost towns' throughout Australia. I recently visited a small town, Merriwagga (near Griffith), in the state of NSW where only 30–40 people (mostly old) live at present, without any young couples or young children in any family. This town remained famous for wheat production until the 1980s, and still serves as a centre for the collection of grain in the region. However, now the town is going to 'disappear' after the current generation passes away.

There are many examples, like Merriwagga, where the younger people have moved out, and old couples only live there because they have been living in these areas for their whole life. The question is how will we manage those farms that are currently being managed by the present (medium-to-older) generation? This is posing some serious consequences, not just for the management of those farms in the future, but also for security and provision of food. It also poses important issues for farmland and conservation area management. If farmland is not managed properly, there are huge consequences and threats for the conservation parks with the spread of weeds and pests, land degradation and loss of biodiversity throughout the country. The environmental costs associated with the management of such threats will be enormous in the future.

If the current scenario continues, our land under cultivation will cease, which will have disastrous consequences for future employment and for maintaining the landscape's natural values. A farmer not only contributes towards food production, but also directly and indirectly helps to maintain the natural landscape for the provision of many ecosystem services to all of us. These ecosystem services could be related to natural beauty, water, education or the provision of habitat for wildlife, all of which directly or indirectly play a significant role in our production systems, as well as in our wellbeing.

If a farmer stops cultivating the land, the whole area will become a target for weeds and pests, which poses a huge threat to many national conservation areas. It has already happened in some national parks. Apart from this, there will be a rise in food costs, the consequences of which we will all experience. I personally feel that we do not value our farmers' efforts in the provision of food and many other services that we all enjoy. Probably we will come to know this when we face food scarcity because of our limited human resources to manage land for production of food.

An alternative approach to farmland management is for big corporations to take over abandoned properties. This has been suggested for some time now. My gut feeling is that the corporate companies will apply a business approach to obtain maximum benefits from land without much emphasis on sustainable use of land or water resources. Whereas, a farmer has much more emotional attachment to the land and farming is much more than just a business for a farmer. I sincerely doubt the efforts of big business corporations to manage the land in the best interests of the environment and people. There will be serious consequences for the Australian public if such a change happens on a large scale.

Climate change is another major threat to the production of food, and hence the provision and security of food in changing climates. Although globally we are mainly responsible for enhancing the effects of climate change (IPCC 2014 and earlier reports), but it is beyond the control of any one person. We all need to act as global citizens. We can't avoid or escape its impact. At this stage, it is important for us to learn to adapt and to cope with the impacts of climate change to reduce its effects on our current farming systems, as well as to reduce the greenhouse gas emissions from farming systems.

Globally, the State of Food Insecurity report by FAO (2008, 2010a) suggests that nearly one billion people suffer from malnutrition in developing countries (Fig. 3.4). This situation will worsen when we include the impacts of climate change. Climate change is projected to affect all the four dimensions of food security: food availability, food accessibility, food utilisation and the stability of food production systems. There will be short-term as well as long-term effects of climate change that will affect rural as well as urban communities.

Undernourishment in 2010, by region (millions)

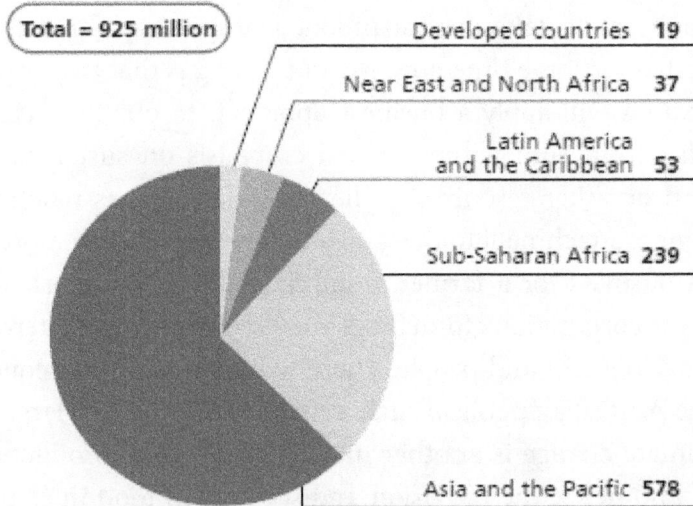

Total = 925 million

Developed countries　19

Near East and North Africa　37

Latin America and the Caribbean　53

Sub-Saharan Africa　239

Asia and the Pacific　578

Fig. 3.4.   Undernourished people by region (Source: The State of Food Insecurity in the World, FAO 2010a).

The changes in climate will not only affect the food production systems, but actually the whole chain from production to supply. People involved at any level of this chain will be adversely affected. These may include loss of opportunities where supply chains are disrupted, increase in market prices, loss of assets and livelihood opportunities, reduction in purchasing power, endangered human health and, at times, the inability of people to cope with the changes in climate. The major concern is that with globalisation we will all face the effects, whether it's happening locally or globally.

Food security

FAO research (FAO 2008, 2010 a and b) suggests that with a change in climate, the security of food for people will be of concern in both developed and developing countries. Agriculture will not only experience the impact of climate change but will also contribute to climate change via greenhouse gas emissions (GHG emissions), along with changes in the social and cultural systems. To date, research has focused mainly on interpreting the impacts of climate change on agricultural systems, not on its impacts on social systems. Researchers do not have predictions as to how people will operate in those severe and insecure circumstances when we face climate adversities more frequently than we face now. I am concerned about human behaviour in such insecure circumstances, although I agree that change in practises as well as different solutions that minimise or mitigate GHG emissions may help us to develop sustainable production systems. We are 'individualistic' societies rather than 'collectivistic' societies, so my concern is that people may not behave so well when we have frequent events of insecurity to our food and water supply.

Our farming systems are largely focused on one type cropping, that is, they are 'monoculture' systems. For example, a crop farmer may produce only wheat while a dairy farmer will produce only milk. Our focus on 'developing economies to scale' has led farmers to adopt a largely mono-cropping and monoculture type of farming approach, which is mainly business-oriented and does not apply the sustainable principles.

It was quite surprising for me to learn when I worked on a grazing property for my doctoral research that the cattle were meant only for beef. There were no cattle to produce milk for the family, despite having so many cattle on the property. The grazier's family had to buy milk from the supermarket, which was initially unusual for me. I often used to think that one could keep a few dairy cows for milk even if it was a beef cattle property. This was in contrast to my childhood experience as mentioned earlier. But later working on pastoral properties in Queensland, the economic viewpoint made me understand that all the farming/grazing is considered from a business perspective rather than from a sustainable perspective. Therefore, it is profitable to keep only beef cattle for the business to maximise financial returns.

However, this is not a sustainable way of living, and it makes us dependent upon external resources to a large extent. To me, it is quite strange that a farmer who produces food for many other people is not self-sufficient for the main food items for his or her family. I would like to think that a cattle property would be able to provide its own meat, as well as milk and cheese, and similarly a grain farm would produce its own grains for bread. By limiting ourselves to only one kind of produce, which may be better in terms of short-term financial returns, we deplete natural resources and limit self-sufficiency of farming communities.

Our farmers and pastoralists are equally dependent upon external resources for their daily food items as an urbanite. Unfortunately, we only experience this heavy dependence on external resources during climate-based calamities such as floods or fire. When roads get cut off, and trucks can't deliver the edible items, many of us feel helpless. If such a situation persists, then food insecurity can lead to serious consequences.

The situation described above is quite in contrast to the farming systems in India where I come from. Even a small farmer (with a land size as small as five acres) can meet the basic needs of the family. I grew up on a reasonable size farm (40 acres of agricultural land) that helped the family to survive and live comfortably. This block of land was enough for four to five family members to live on since the land was fertile and productive. There is intensive agriculture on this type of farm that involves a lot of human efforts. The farm produce included food such as wheat, rice, maize, sugarcane, fodder for the dairy cattle/buffaloes, legumes (mung beans), and some seasonal vegetables, and was also able to generate a good income from the commercial sale of wheat and rice. This kind of farming system at least helps people to be self-sufficient by supplying most of their food items and enabling them to survive through hard times. In contrast, the 'economies of scale' farming systems in Australia help to generate income, but as I discussed earlier, do not enhance farming families to be self-sufficient or sustainable over the long term.

The current monoculture farming systems are based on financial returns to match the economies of scale for maximum returns. The focus is on financial profitability, not on the capability of the system to be sustainable. There are exceptions where Australian farmers are doing things differently to develop sustainable farming systems, but their numbers are few.

Food security is an important issue that links to our social behaviour, and it impacts all of us, whether rural or urban. The Australian government defines food security as 'when populations have access on an ongoing basis to sufficient, safe and nutritious food to meet their dietary needs and food preferences for an active and healthy life' (The Australian Government, AusAid).

With the change in climate and the way our modern farming systems are set up, we are all prone to food insecurity (discussed in the next section). Although we have enough produce because food is produced at different places at larger scales, we may all suffer if transport failure occurs in delivering the food to the required places. This will impact people of all ages, including children, adults and elders. If catastrophic events become too frequent, as is projected for the Australian climate (Garnaut 2008, Hennessya et al. 2008, State of Climate 2012 and 2014), it will also bring changes in people's social behaviour including their attitude of treating each other with tolerance or their ability to support each other. This may further lead to greater insecurity, particularly when people may not be used to the insecure environment. Coping with climatic events is going to be difficult, providing food to people will be just one of the difficulties. For example, the Queensland floods in 2011 largely disturbed the provision of food in many areas in South East Queensland. And this happened again in 2013 when people felt devastated by consecutive events within a gap of just two years. There were still many people who had not recovered well after the 2011 floods and then the 2013 floods really ruined them. I wonder how much we can support such people as a community if these events are too frequent. With climate change, we can expect these kinds of events are going to be more frequent and vast, and we may not be able to cope with the provision of food and other items. This may lead to further problems and issues on a social scale, depending upon how well a community is capable of withstanding the adversities of nature.

At a global scale, the anticipated increase in the world population (9 billion by 2050) also suggests food insecurity in the future (Fig. 3.5). The number of under-nourished people (approximately 900 million) constitutes a large part of our global population. Despite all the advances in agriculture, not all the people in the world have access to good food. As the world population increases, the situation will worsen as most land has already been used for cultivation, and there will not be much left for agricultural expansion.

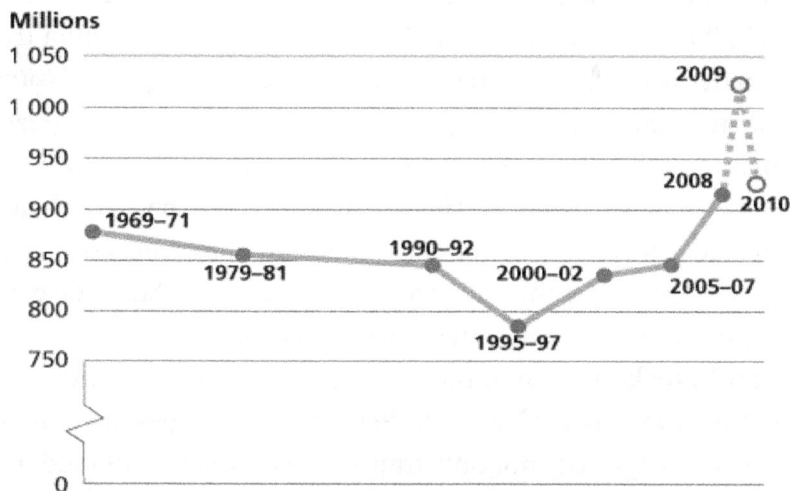

Millions

1 050	
1 000	2009
950	
900	2008 2010
850	1969–71
800	1990–92
750	1979–81 2000–02 2005–07
0	1995–97

Note: Figures for 2009 and 2010 are estimated by FAO with input from   *Source:* FAO.
the United States Department of Agriculture, Economic Research Service.
Full details of the methodology are provided in the technical background
notes (available at www.fao.org/publication/sofi/en/).

*Fig. 3.5:   Number of under-nourished people in the world,
1969-71 to 2010 (Source: FAO 2010).*

Impacts of climate change on food security

We mostly know that mean global temperatures have been increasing since about 1950, mainly due to accumulation of greenhouse gases such as carbon dioxide, nitrous oxide and methane in the atmosphere (IPCC reports 2014 and earlier). Anthropogenic factors are the main causes for the increase in concentration of these gases and consequently, the increase in temperatures. Among the other factors, the burning of fossil fuels (coal, oil and gas) to meet our increasing energy demand, and the spread of intensive agriculture to meet increasing food demand which is often accompanied by deforestation (FAO 2008), are the two major anthropogenic causes for current changes in the climate.

The process of global warming is now experienced all over the world and is expected to bring long-term changes in weather conditions (FAO 2008). Around the world, there is a growing recognition that, no matter what steps are taken to control greenhouse gas emissions now, we need action to prepare for the likely impacts of greater climate variability and for the changes occurring in our climate (World Resources 2010-11). This is mainly because there are already increased concentrations of these gases in the atmosphere that will exert their warming effect for decades to come. So, to save our natural and agricultural systems, we need to act now.

Firstly, we know that our food production systems (agriculture, fisheries and forestry) are all sensitive to changes in climate. Climate change does not only impact the production of food, but it also impacts food accessibility, food availability, food utilisation and food systems' stability (FAO 2008). This means that the agricultural production system and its ability to produce food could decline. Even if enough food is produced, it may become unavailable to people due to threatening climate conditions. This has happened during recent floods in Australia where some commodities such as milk, bread, etc. were not accessible where people needed them the most.

The impacts of climate change on food systems are not just limited to the rural areas where food is produced, but it will be evident both in rural and urban communities. The urban areas, where 80 per cent of the population lives in Australia, may experience unavailability of food due to a disrupted food chain or rise in food prices. This could lead to serious health consequences.

Moreover, scientific evidence suggests more frequent and intense weather events such as cyclones, droughts, heavy storms and floods, rising sea levels and increasing irregularities in rainfall will all significantly impact food production systems, as well as the distribution and access to food at many places around the world. Severe weather conditions will also impact other assets related to agricultural production systems, and on the spread of pests and diseases. Overall, climate change will have severe impacts not just on the production systems, but also on the availability and accessibility of food, and consequently, on the social and cultural systems that demand a detailed study.

Australian scenario on climate change

The State of Climate Report (2012) by the Australian Bureau of Meteorology (BOM) projects that each decade has been warmer than the previous decade since the 1950s. Moreover, the Australian annual average daily mean temperatures have shown little change from 1910 to 1950 but have progressively warmed since 1950, increasing by 0.9°C from 1910 to 2011 (Fig. 3.6). The average temperature during the past 10 years has been more than 0.5°C warmer than the World Meteorological Organisation's standard 1961–1990 long-term average. This increase continues the trend observed since the 1950s of each decade being warmer than the previous one. A major concern is that such increases in temperature (1°C rise) are quite widespread throughout the continent, particularly in the eastern region from the north to the south (Fig. 3.7).

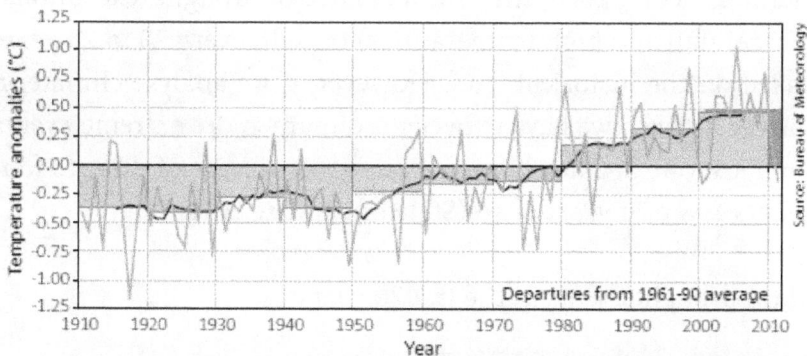

Fig. 3.6:   Changes in the Australian climate: temperature and anomalies since 1910 (source: State of Climate (2012) — Bureau of Meteorology).

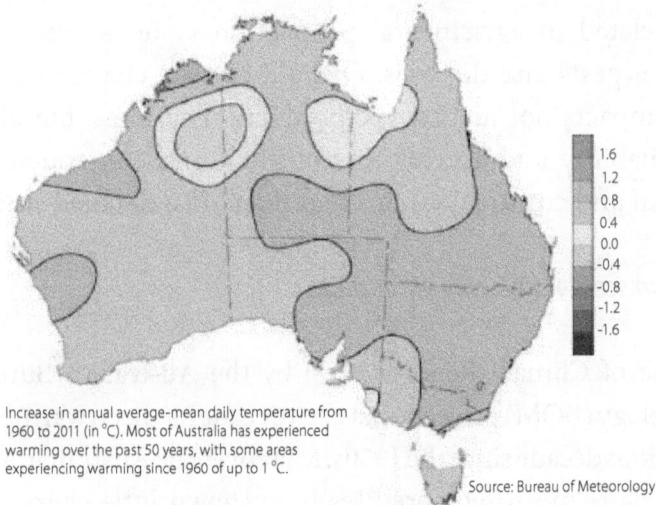

Increase in annual average-mean daily temperature from 1960 to 2011 (in °C). Most of Australia has experienced warming over the past 50 years, with some areas experiencing warming since 1960 of up to 1 °C.

Source: Bureau of Meteorology

Fig. 3.7:   Australian Map of Changes in Annual Average Mean Temperatures from 1960-2011 (Source: Bureau of Meteorology).

Regarding the twentieth-century Australian climate, the Bureau of Meteorology (BOM) summarised it as: 'Droughts, dust and deluge — a century of climate extremes in Australia' (BOM website).

As per the climate assessment by the BOM and CSIRO (Commonwealth Scientific Industrial and Research Organisation; Hennessy et al. 2008), there is a chance of drought (exceptional low rainfall and high temperatures) once in every 20 to 25 years based on the historical data. However, if we analyse climate in the recent past, we have experienced many more extreme events than just one in 20 to 25 years, indeed an average of three to four events every 20 years or so (State of Climate 2014).

Main drought events in the last 20 years:

- 1982–83: Large areas of central and south-east Australia 1982–83 experienced exceptionally low rainfall.
- 1991–95: North-Eastern NSW and many parts in Queensland experienced drought because of low rainfall levels.

- 2002–2006: Eastern and southern Australia experienced widespread drought.
- 2012: Southern parts of Australia experienced drought (SA).
- Floods and cyclones:
- 1990: Severe floods in Queensland and NSW, with the towns Charleville and Nyngan being the most affected.
- 2006: Cyclone Larry damages many parts of Far North Queensland.
- 2010: Cyclone Yasi hits the Far North Queensland coast.
- 2010–11: Severe floods in southern Queensland.
- 2012: Floods in NSW.
- 2013: Severe floods in southeast Queensland.

Impact of Tropical Cyclone Larry

In March 2006, the far north Queensland coast was declared a natural disaster zone after experiencing the impact of Tropical Cyclone Larry.

Cyclone Larry was classified as a category five cyclone and created winds of up to 290 km/h. It destroyed banana plantations within a 40 to 50 kilometre radius of the cyclone path and caused huge damage to banana crops in the area, leaving many parts of Australia without bananas and the price of the fruit rocketed in the markets. The total estimated cost for the damage was $1.5 billion.

Apart from damage to the food crops, I have witnessed the damage to the natural systems that were devastated by this event. It could take years for those systems to come back to original state, if it happens to be (actually the weeds and fast growing plants tend to occupy the open spaces first, and changes the vegetation composition of the area). With changes in vegetation composition, the faunal diversity is expected to change as well. The impacts of such events on the socio-ecological system for people in the region are enormous and are difficult to fully investigated. However, people in North Queensland are quite resilient, and they have learnt to live with such events to some extent.

Extreme weather events like cyclones can adversely affect the availability and cost of fresh food. In 2005, poor weather and higher fuel costs increased the prices of potatoes, broccoli, onions, tomatoes and other varieties of fruit. Furthermore, the scientists have warned that more cyclones like Larry will form if no action is taken against climate change. Cyclones obtain their energy from warm tropical seas. The warmer the ocean, the greater the intensity of the cyclone. Climate change has been shown to increase sea temperatures (IPCC 2014 and earlier reports) which will contribute to increases in cyclonic events.

Occurrence of extreme weather events has increased significantly over the last 20 years. Extreme events are occurring not just once in 20 to 25 years, but rather once in every five to 10 years. If such events become more frequent, there will be failures in production systems and disruptions in the distribution of food items. With changes in climate, we need to adapt ourselves to the changes that could occur in food production systems so that they minimally affect our living.

Australian food security and climate change

According to a report by the Prime Minister's Science, Engineering and Innovation Council (PMSEIC 2010), Australian food security is inextricably linked to political stability and presently the likelihood of a food crisis appears very remote. We produce enough food today to feed 60 million people and, therefore, can export food to other parts of the world. Our main challenges for food production and the stability of the systems are (PMSEIC 2010):

1. Vulnerability to the change in climate.
2. Land degradation and decline in soil fertility coupled with the loss of productive land in outer-urban regions due to urban development.
3. In relation to climate change, agriculture is a major sector responsible for emitting greenhouse gases (Fig. 3.8).

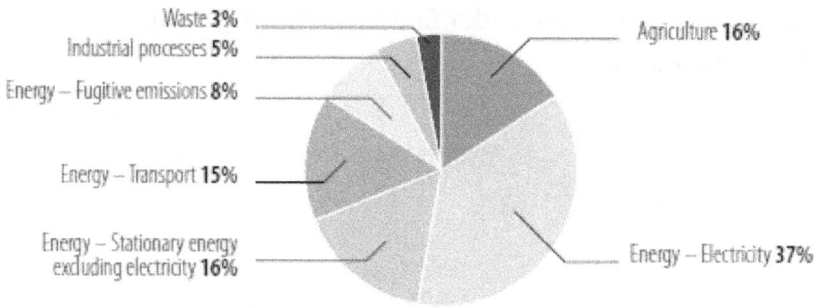

Waste 3%
Industrial processes 5%
Energy – Fugitive emissions 8%
Energy – Transport 15%
Energy – Stationary energy excluding electricity 16%
Agriculture 16%
Energy – Electricity 37%

Fig. 3.8: *Australian Greenhouse Gas Emissions by Sector (Source: PMSEIC Report 2010).*

On a global scale, Australia contributes significantly to the food security through maintaining its leading position for producing food on the driest continent in the world with low-quality soils and in the face of continuing climate variability.

Since our food is readily available and is of good quality, we do not pay much attention to this great service. Food production is quite challenging on this dry continent mainly due to ancient and infertile soils, variability in soil types and climate, and in many cases, harsh climates and significant land degradation from soil erosion, acidification and salinisation. Despite all these factors, a culture of innovation, research and development in the agriculture sector has led us to develop efficient production systems.

Water availability and climate variability are the two major factors that determine agricultural production in Australia. A drought year can reduce wheat production by up to 60 per cent or more compared to a good year. We need to realise how our farming systems are being managed, and how to make them sustainable, not necessarily from a profit perspective but from a long-term sustainable gains perspective that can help communities survive for the centuries to come. I believe that every little effort counts. If we start realising the value of food produced in such harsh environments, I believe we will also implement changes in our ways of living that help us to live sustainably.

Cassava and Cyanide Under Elevated Atmospheric Carbon Dioxide

As atmospheric carbon dioxide increases, it has been demonstrated that the nutrition levels of many plants decrease and, for some, the levels of toxins increase. This may present serious problems when trying to feed an increasing population under the conditions of climate change.

Cassava is a staple crop for more than 750 million people worldwide. Both the tuber and the leaves are edible. The tubers are the main food product and are toxic unless carefully processed. All parts of the plant contain cyanogenic glycosides. These serve as a defence mechanism against pests by breaking down to poisonous cyanide gas if the leaves are crushed or chewed. The leaves must be carefully prepared to liberate the gas or those who consume it risk developing a lifelong paralysis, known as konzo.

Under elevated atmospheric carbon dioxide, cassava plants allocate more resources to defence, so the cyanogenic glycosides in the leaves increase and protein content decreases. Furthermore, the increased defence comes at the cost of decreased tuber yields.

By 2050, it is estimated that nearly one billion people will rely on cassava. In the next 20 to 30 years, scientists will need to develop cultivars that will show a different response to increased carbon dioxide concentrations (Gleadow et al. 2009 a and b).

There are recent reports in various agriculture journals that even the protein in our main cereal, wheat, is less when grown under higher concentrations of greenhouse gases. Overall, the quality of food grown under greater concentrations of greenhouse gases is expected to deteriorate.

Climate variability is a part of the Australian continent. As it's commonly said, 'Australia is indeed a land of droughts and flooding rains' (PMSEIC 2010). We need to learn to adapt ourselves to our changing climates and to adapt the ability of our systems to produce food.

Despite the scientific evidence, available information and experience of farmers and common people in Australia, the current Government is not actively admitting climate change as a risk to our food production systems. This appears a short-term limited vision. There is an urgent need to look at the long-term perspective given that the Australian continent is prone to droughts, fires, floods and cyclones, so we do seriously need to safeguard our food systems for long-term gains in the future.

Climate change, food security and a way forward

After reading such a long section on food security and climate change, one would wonder what could possibly be done to reduce the impact. How can we adapt ourselves to climate changes and the resulting changes in food availability and our food preferences?

Although, acclimatisation to climate change is a good strategy, we also really need to learn to mitigate climate change and make every effort to save our planet. In the meantime while we are facing the impacts of previous acts, we can focus on adaptation and improving the system for the future. How can we change our attitudes towards the use and value of natural resources that will help us to adapt to the change?

A few simple strategies that could be applicable at a household scale are:

1. Try to embed yourself a little within nature. It may be difficult for urban populations, but it is possible. This could be achieved by growing herbs and other food plants at a household scale, and learning to value products produced at home. This could also be possible by reducing barriers with nature e.g. preferring natural climate (not using Air Conditioning), producing less waste, etc. It can provide a sense of achievement that it is possible to contribute to reducing the greenhouse gas emissions.

2. We should make efforts to lessen the impacts of climate change, at least in the short term. This could be achieved by planting trees or bushes, reducing the use of cars, using less electricity and/or by applying green energy techniques such as solar panels and windmills and by using energy-efficient tools.

3. Making effective use of resources such as fuel, electricity and gas, etc. This includes changes in our current habits and attitudes. For example, using a car only when needed or practising judicial use of electricity by every member of a household.

4. Using a bicycle or walking for short distances.

5. Generating less waste and recycling materials including our green waste.

6. Strengthening our resilience and adjusting our food habits to the changes in food systems (building climate-friendly food habits).

7. Learning about promoting sustainable ways of living.

8. Minimising resource use by accumulating only necessary household items.

9. Above all, realising the value of resources and services from our natural systems and embedding ourselves within nature as a part of the whole system.

Sustainable living certainly requires changes in our current attitude and values as well as in strengthening our capacity to adapt to natural conditions. Individual, as well as social efforts, can play a significant role in how we value and use our natural resources.

Recently, I witnessed a good example of how people are capable of adapting to change quickly. It was a very hot summer day (35°C) in Toowoomba, Queensland, and probably most people had their air conditioning on. People didn't have the capacity to tolerate the hot weather, and thus air conditioning was most useful. By the afternoon, there was an electricity problem in the city due to the overuse of power, and it was at first a 'brownout' (where parts of some houses had no electricity) and later a total 'blackout'. It is important to note that summer is usually mild in Toowoomba with a daily maximum temperature of 27°C. There is always a cool breeze even on very hot days, especially at night when the temperatures drop to 10–15°C.

The social perspective of such an event is still memorable for me. When it was a total blackout at night, some people came out in our street. We could hear voices outside when usually our street is quiet. There was a rather lively feeling to the street, and people had their own resources such as torches, to cope with the lack of electricity. I guess this short-lived experience did make some of us realise that hot days are a part of the natural climate in this region, and we need to adapt ourselves to such a change by learning and doing things that are in harmony with nature. It was a good demonstration, for children, as well as for adults, that electricity is a precious resource, and it showed how we can adapt to not having such a resource at least for a short while. Also, it provided an opportunity for social interaction.

In such circumstances, there is a lot to learn about how we can adapt to climate changes, in terms of our individual as well as social responses. Some of these learnings reinforce the idea of the benefit of changes in our attitudes on resource use and value, food habits and ways of living (e.g. eco-friendly housing). In some ways, Indigenous knowledge can provide us with some guidance on how we can better adapt for future living.

Indigenous knowledge

In the past, Australia's Indigenous people lived with nature since their food was totally derived from the natural resources of their surroundings, and they were very familiar with the changes in the climate. They used trees and bushes as symbols (eco-friendly) where the flowering of a particular tree or change in the color of leaves of a tree indicated that a particular type of food would be available in certain areas at certain times. They linked their lives to nature because they were totally dependent upon natural resources for various benefits and uses that they needed.

I believe there is a need to embed knowledge from Indigenous Australians into our current knowledge systems. The Indigenous knowledge of natural systems is invaluable, but unfortunately not much progress has been made to integrate this knowledge with the western (modern) knowledge, or to record and embed this knowledge into everyday use in Australia. In many instances, there is scientific rationale behind Indigenous practises, especially when analysed from an ecological and conservation science perspective. Unfortunately, we are losing traditional knowledge very rapidly. It is regretful that we, the general public, hardly know any uses of the native trees and bushes that surround us (with few exceptions). We hardly see any native fruit or herbs for use in our supermarkets (except for the macadamia nut which was first cultivated and made popular by the Hawaiians).

Integrating use of native plants in our daily lives should be our next step. It can help us in a number of ways to develop sustainable living while adapting to climate change. For example, native flora and fauna are expected to be more adaptable to the local climate than any other exotic plants, and it may have greater levels of resilience. In severe events, knowledge of local flora and fauna may prove useful for food and medicine, and for recreational, health or spiritual benefits. The non-Indigenous population needs to at least learn how to use some native plants and how to grow the commonly used plants. Growing native bushes, trees and herbs and making use of them in our daily lives, will help us to comprehend the impact of changes in the climate on these plants, and thus will emphasise the need to adapt ourselves to the change that is fast approaching.

The Indigenous approach towards natural resources, being a part of the system (country or land), is something we all need to embrace in the modern world. Indigenous people highly value their connections to country and will often say we belong to that country. Whereas, non-Indigenous people will often say that we own that piece of land. This change in attitude to incorporating some traditional values will be useful not just for us but also for the future generations.

4. Waste

Apart from the overuse or misuse of resources mentioned above, another major concern is waste production. We produce a lot of waste at a household scale. If we want to live in harmony with nature, we need to figure out ways to reduce our waste production and to use our resources efficiently.

The high volume of waste produced in Australia is becoming a major environmental concern (ABS 2009, 2010). In fact, Australians are among the world's largest producers of waste. After the US, Australia produces more waste per person each year than the inhabitants of any other continent. Each person in Australia creates nearly 1 to 2 tonnes of household waste every year. The Australian Bureau of Statistics (2010) reported that in 2001, 19 million tonnes of waste were dumped into landfills, and by 2007 this figure had grown to 21.3 million tonnes, a 12 per cent increase (ABS 2010). Imagine if there was 1 to 2 tonnes of garbage lying in everyone's backyard by the end of every year!

Plastic bags make up the bulk of the waste we produce. Nearly a trillion bags per year are used and discarded worldwide, and up to 7 billion of these bags are from Australia. Most plastic bags are made from oil or gas products and do not easily break down. It can actually take from 20 to 100 years for a plastic bag to fully decompose. The oil used to produce just nine plastic bags can run a car for a distance of nearly 1 kilometre.

Among all the Australian States (2006–07; ABS 2010-Environmental Trends and Issues), New South Wales (NSW) produced the most waste at approximately 15,000 tonnes, followed by Victoria (approximately 10,000 tonnes) and Queensland (approximately 8000 tonnes). Whereas, the other states produced much less waste such as South Australia with approximately 3000 tonnes, and Australian Capital Territory (ACT), Northern Territory (NT) and Tasmania, that each produced approximately 1000 tonnes. However, these figures are dependent on population density. In terms of per capita waste, Western Australia, followed by ACT and NSW produced the most waste of about approximately 2400, 2300 and 2200 kg/person, respectively. All the other states produced waste of about 2000 kg/person (ABS 2010 — Environmental Trends and Issues).

Let's look at the major components of our household waste: these are plastic bags, bottles, glass materials, cardboards, paper and other solid waste that enters the landfill every week or so. I wonder if the council trucks did not turn up every week, it would be a chaotic situation to manage the waste in many households. Supermarkets are also a major source of waste. A typical supermarket's waste is made up of 46 per cent packaged food and 27 per cent unpackaged food (Fig. 3.9).

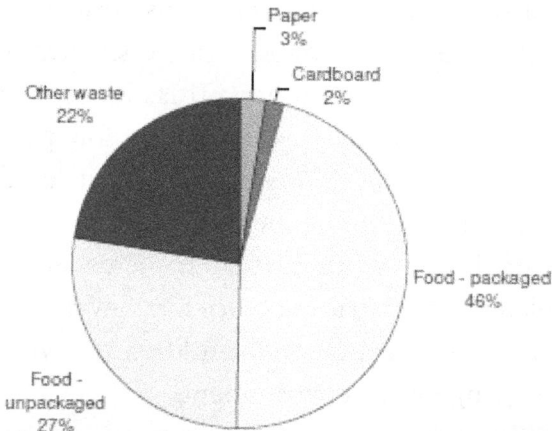

Fig. 3.9:   Breakdown of waste from a typical supermarket
             (Source: Oke et al. (2009) Waste and Recycling
             in Australia 2009, a report prepared by Hyder
             Consulting).

To reduce the amount of waste we produce, we need to understand why we create so much waste in the first place. Often, we throw away items that can be easily reused. Our attitudes need to change in order for us to achieve a sustainable future for ourselves and for future generations. According to the Department of Environment and Heritage Protection, most of our waste is created when:

1. We go food shopping and use plastic bags to carry produce, and then, at the checkout counter, we pack our purchases in plastic bags again.
2. Many supermarkets now provide recycling bins for plastic bags, but most customers do not use them.
3. Many food items in supermarkets are packed in paper or plastic two to three times. For example, fruit bars are

often packed in a wrapper and then in a cardboard box. Similarly, the packaging for chips, biscuits, and many other items includes double wrappers which are used for the convenience of consumers. This practice has two major disadvantages. Firstly, it wastes paper, foil, plastic, etc., on packaging. Secondly, it misuses space that could be used to fit more products on the shelves.

4. For schoolchildren, in particular, items such as biscuits, chocolates, etc. are packed twice for convenience, although this double packaging sends children the wrong message about caring for the environment.

5. Meat and other items are often packed in foam trays and plastics.

6. We throw away so many items that can be reused, repurposed, recycled or composted.

7. We have become accustomed to pretty yet wasteful packaging.

8. We overuse resources to produce goods that meet market standards with a lot of unnecessary materials used during the packaging process.

9. In addition to plastic waste, liquid waste (e.g., sewage runoff, household detergents, and industrial chemicals) causes major problems for our environment. Most liquid wastewater is disposed of in coastal regions, and only about 1 per cent is recycled.

Recycling waste materials

There are generally two different approaches to recycling. The first approach involves creating a lot of recyclable waste and then recycling it. This is a common *modus operandi* of Australians and many other people living in developed countries. The other approach involves generating fewer recyclable materials and recycling minimally or not at all.

For example, milk is a common purchase for many of us, and

we buy it from supermarkets in plastic bottles. We need it every week, and at the end of each month, the average family wastes 100–150 bottles of plastic, just by purchasing milk. If the same family keeps up this pace, there will be 1200–1800 bottles wasted by the end of the year.

There are many other plastic items such as bottles for cold drinks and water. For many of us, the number of these bottles may be twice as many as the milk bottles so we can account for 2000 bottles per year. Over a year, an average small-sized family of four members wastes approximately 4000 bottles. This is a huge amount of waste, and the irony is that there are alternatives. For example, in the city of Burlington in Vermont (US), some academics and local organisations brought a change in the government policy that allowed the local dairy farmers to sell milk directly to the public. So, the locals bought milk from the farmers using glass/steel bottles or containers that were re-used. Similarly, in India the milk vendors sell milk to the locals on a daily basis and people use their own steel/ glass containers to store the milk (although this trend has changed in metropolitan cities and is rapidly changing at many places due to the availability of packaged milk in plastic containers).

No doubt that in developed countries, people generate a heap of waste materials and then count on recycling to protect the environment. I would like to point out that not all materials are recyclable. Additionally, recycling itself involves use of energy and also generates waste.

In 2006–07, a total of 43,777,000 tonnes of waste were generated in Australia, and 22,707,000 tonnes (52 per cent of Australia's waste) was recycled (National Waste Report, 2010). Of this waste:

- 42 per cent was from the construction and demolition waste stream,
- 36 per cent was from the commercial and industrial waste stream, and
- 22 per cent was from the municipal waste stream.

Our per capita production of waste of 1000 kg per person is extremely high and in essence, we recycle only 5 per cent of our total waste per capita (National Waste Report, 2010).

Reusing waste materials out of necessity

In the marketplaces in India, plastic bags are reused and recycled in many different ways. Plastic bags, as well as old clothes and rags, are often used to make mats, stools and baskets. Families often sell used newspapers, which are then used to make many other products.

In India, waste management is a major issue, but at the household level, people frequently recycle various waste materials.

In the marketplace, shoppers bring their own reusable bags to carry vegetables and other groceries. Usually, vegetables and fruits come fresh from the local farmers to a vegetable market, and people come to buy them throughout the week. It is habit usually to take your own cotton bag. Also people do tend to use a resource a bit more efficiently as not many resources are readily available for use. Overall, although management of the waste and population are big issues there, at a small household level, people have their own techniques to recycle the waste as shown below.

Minimising the use of plastic:
A lesson from a US organic market

I saw a unique approach to minimise the amount of plastic used in food shopping at an organic grocery store. In this store, many food items, including grains, cereals, beans, etc. were kept in large containers without any packaging. Customers only used plastic or paper bags to carry what they needed. In fact, many of the customers did not use plastic bags at all.

How the disposal of waste can harm the environment

We use plastic bags and other items so often that it is difficult for us to be without plastic materials. The major environmental harm of these plastics is that they may take many years to decompose. For example, some items such as nappies can take up to 250–500 years or plastic bags about 20–1000 years to decompose, depending upon the quality of the material. Accumulation of these materials in drainage pipes, terrestrial and marine systems and in the animal food chain are some of the major concerns.

Although we recycle some of our waste, half of it still ends up in the landfill. The problem with landfill waste is that it does not biodegrade quickly. Instead, garbage sits there for years and creates more waste in the form of methane gas and waste water. If you ever happen to pass by a landfill site, the smell is unforgettable. Gases from landfills contain poisonous chemicals that are dangerous to the environment.

Greenhouse gases from a landfill.

Waste emissions from the landfill sites are predominantly methane (CH_4) and account for less than 3 per cent of Australia's total emissions. In 2007, we had total waste emissions approximately 14.6 Mt CO_2-e (ABS 2010). Moreover, it is wastage of land potential that could be used for other purposes. With increases in population and levels of wastage production per capita, the increase in the number of landfill sites is a serious concern.

Composting — Putting organic waste to good use

One major concern is the production of organic waste, which can be used as fertiliser for gardens but ends up in landfills. This waste can be used for our vegetable gardens, which would reduce greenhouse gas emissions from landfills. Recycling organic waste depends entirely on people's interest and attitudes. It is really easy to recycle organic waste. Simply purchase a bin specifically meant for your food scraps and leave your organic waste to decompose. Whatever remains can be used to fertilise your garden. Composting not only reduces the amount of waste that we produce, but it also reduces the production of greenhouse gases and saves the money that we would spend on fertilisers.

The good news is that more and more people are beginning to compost. Since 2007, nearly 65 per cent of households have been recycling organic waste (ABS 2010, Australia's Environment — Issues and Trends). This is something we all must do!

Recycling efficiency: how much do we actually recycle?

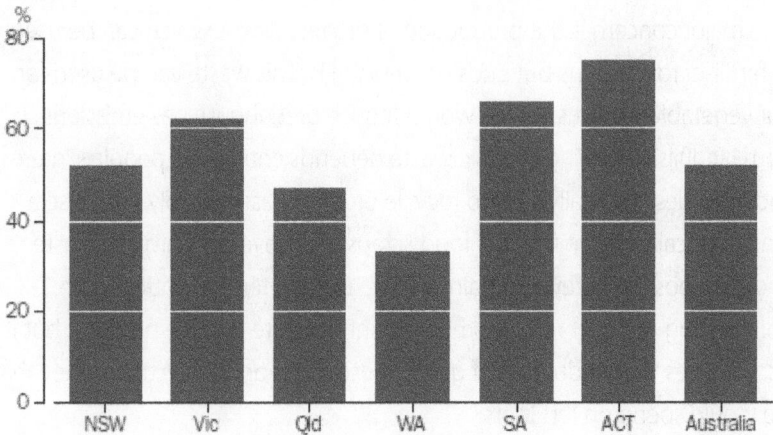

Fig. 3.10: Percentage of total waste recycled, by State, 2006–07 (Source: Environmental Protection and Heritage Council (EPHC) (2009) report on National Waste Overview).

The average recycling rate in Australia for 2006–07 was about 52 per cent, but it varied between states and territories. While the Australian Capital Territory recycled most of its waste (three-quarters of the waste it generated) (Fig. 3.10), it still had the second highest per capita rate of waste production in Australia. Western Australia recycled only one-third of its waste while it generated the maximum amount of waste per capita in Australia. From the Australian Capital Territory example, we can see that producing lots of waste and then recycling it can help to reduce levels of waste to some extent. Still, it would be much more efficient to produce less waste and then recycle whatever is possible.

E-Waste

Among various kinds of waste materials, e-waste is a major concern these days. In 2007–08, 31.7 million new televisions, computers, and computer products were sold in Australia. Another 16.8 million units reached the end of their life that year. Of these, 88 per cent ended up in landfills.

It's becoming a major problem in almost all the developed countries of the world, and there are not yet any readily available solutions to handle this waste.

Changing our attitudes: produce large amounts of waste and then recycle?

In the modern world, people have access to an abundance of resources, which has led to the present generation's 'use and throw away' attitude. We have developed the inefficient habit of producing mountains of waste and then recycling it. By doing this, we are ultimately wasting our resources and energy. So, what can we do about it?

Applying a dual action strategy: producing less waste and recycling our waste efficiently

We could be well ahead of many other continents in the world if we commit to producing less waste and recycling the waste we produce as efficiently as possible.

Reducing the amount of waste we generate involves making major changes in our habits and attitudes surrounding the use of plastics and other materials. Currently, we use products that generate a lot of waste and then we recycle them and boast about how we are living in an environmentally sustainable way. Why do we first create a huge amount of waste and then spend energy and resources recycling that waste?

If we took stock of our daily activities, we would see that there are many occasions where we could completely avoid the use of plastic bottles, bags, etc. Often we do not even need to use plastics at all. If we could take the next step and change these wasteful habits, we could help save the environment.

Actions to reduce waste

1. Buy items not wrapped in plastic.
2. Buy fruits and vegetables without putting them in plastic bags, if possible, otherwise use cloth bags.
3. Opt out of using plastic when purchasing bottles of milk or water.
4. Avoid using items that are wrapped in plastics.
5. At home, try to minimise the use of plastic wrap and aluminium foil. Instead, choose reusable containers to pack your lunches and snacks.
6. Use reusable containers for your beverages.
7. Buy items sold in bulk instead of small, pre-packaged items.
8. Teach your children by setting an example to minimise the amount of waste.

To conclude this chapter, we looked at our attitudes and habits towards resource use, particularly for paper, water, waste production and food. We discussed in detail food security, climate change and its implications for our farming systems and the impacts of climate change on food security from a global and Australian perspective. We interrogated ourselves for current resource use, wastage habits and then we tried to come up with some solutions for how we can change our attitude for a sustainable living that can enhance our connections with the natural resources.

Overall, to live sustainably, we all need to change our attitudes to thinking collectively, using resources in an efficient way, getting away from the habit of accumulating items (think before you buy a new item), better adapting to our surroundings and doing our best as a global citizen to make Earth a better place; not just for the present but also for the future generations of all living organisms, to live and enjoy life for the times to come.

4

Economic world

'There is more to life than increasing its speed.'

— Mahatma Gandhi

The term 'economics' is usually used to reflect money-related issues, finances, income, commodities and material wealth. However, if we broaden our thinking, economics is not all about the flow of money in an economy, it includes many non-monetary aspects as well. This chapter focuses on exploring such non-monetary aspects of economics (i.e. soft core economics) in terms of human wellbeing and its links to the natural resources.

The word 'economics' is made up of two words: 'eco' meaning 'household', and 'nomics' meaning management. Thus, 'economics' means 'management of the household'. Economics is largely perceived as 'choices' at all levels of society, that is, choices by the individuals, by the societies, by the firms and by the governments. By making choices, we attempt to maximise our satisfaction or utility. The words 'choices' and 'utility' are commonly used in the economics literature. For example, we make a choice to keep parkland in the middle of the city or to develop that land for shops, but whatever we choose to do, we intend to maximise the utility of that land. In a broad sense, economics is the study of how we choose to allocate scarce resources among alternative uses in the pursuit of given objectives.

Our choices largely depend upon our level of knowledge in

relation to interpreting the benefits and costs or consequences of our actions. Mostly, we realise the effects after the actions have been taken or after we lose a resource. This is the most common situation with our natural resources. Firstly, we use the resource and once it is used or over-used and/or exploited, then we realise the importance of that resource. We *utilise* the resource so as to *maximise its utility* rather than to *optimise the utility*. If we focus on *optimising* our utilities, we can live better while caring for the environment we live in. Unfortunately, it is a common human tendency to maximise and extract the possible benefits, and to value something when it is scarce.

Our knowledge and understanding can play a significant role in interpreting the after-effects of loss of resources, in other words, its utility, in advance. We can do so by identifying the loss of resources and its related benefits by calculating the costs and benefits of foregone resources for the individuals and for the society in advance. We can also interpret the loss of these resources in terms of the wellbeing of people. This is a very important aspect in the economics of natural resources, where generally we try to estimate the value or benefit of a resource once a resource is exploited or used up. But we can't replace it once it is already over-used, or it is gone. Interestingly, in our modern day-to-day life we do not hear much about the economics of our natural resources — what is their status (increasing or decreasing), or what is the worth of our natural capital?

Mostly, we hear about macro-economics in the news that often present figures concerned with larger scale economics or how the economy as a whole works. For example, in the agriculture sector, macro-economics provides information about total agricultural production in a country (including various commodities, markets, labour costs etc.), and the value of export and import of various items in the sector. We can apply a similar approach at the household level. For example, we can explore the links between our household economy and macro/industrial economy as these are linked to each other, as shown below (Fig. 4.1):

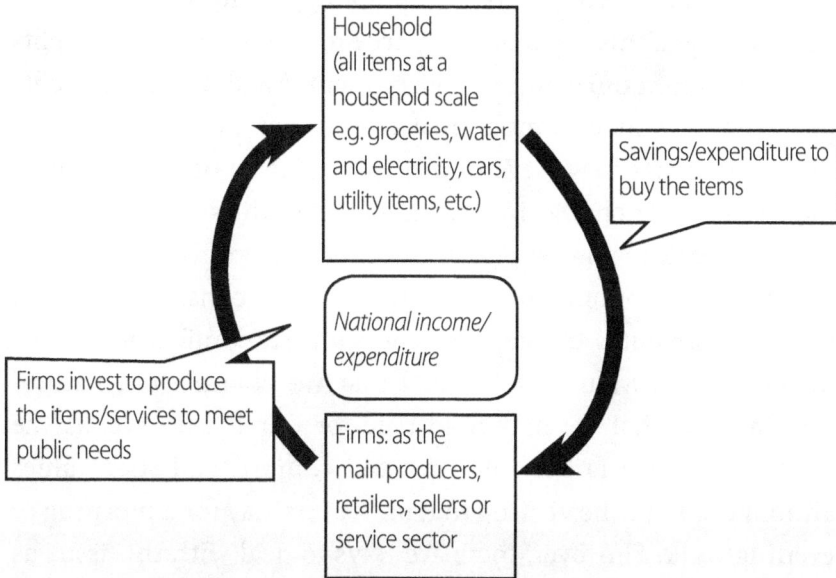

Fig. 4.1.   A simple model to show the flow of macro-economy.

Each and every household plays a significant role in the aggregate economy, or in what we call the macro-economy. Macro-economy includes indicators such as Gross Domestic Product (GDP) that we hear often in the news or the trends in employment, inflation, consumption or savings, share values or price indices that are commonly presented. However, these financial reports fail to tell us the value of our natural capital, increasing/decreasing — we don't hear about the value or status of our natural resources at all.

For the purpose of this book, we will focus on economics at the household scale, particularly on the use, benefits and costs of natural resources in our daily lives. This type of economics is a part of micro-economics in the economics discipline. Our natural resources are indeed the basis of micro- and macro- economics. Without the natural resources, our economies cannot run!

As a measurement stick, money is a useful tool and implied for most items we deal with in our economic lives. However, there are many such items where we do not apply any such measures or 'price tags'. This is particularly true for the services or benefits we obtain from our natural environment. Most of these benefits go unnoticed in our modern economy, we don't hear in the media/financial news, even once in a quarter of a year. There may be a loss or change in a natural asset such as a national park or a city park for development or other reasons, but it does not make to our economic news. There is limited consideration how a park contributes to people's lives. Our economic system fails to incorporate values or benefits that we obtain from natural systems and that we may hold true for our living. We, as the main users, also fail to interpret and comprehend such values although we may be visiting that park every day for a morning or evening walk. However, there are ways to deal with this issue as mentioned later in this chapter.

We should understand now that our natural systems, such as rainforests, woodlands or grasslands or semi-natural/altered systems, play a significant role in running the economic 'money circle'. These systems are inter-connected and provide us with services and benefits such as recreation, education, grazing lands for cattle and sheep, and agricultural/cropping land for grains and other crops and fruits that all contribute to human wellbeing. Nevertheless, the role of natural resources is usually hidden in the economy's bigger picture. We account only for the main commodities, such as crops, but we usually do not consider the other systems (natural systems and their ecosystem services) that play a vital role in the production of those commodities, such as the benefits of pollination, provision of water or diversity of flora and fauna.

Unfortunately, most of our development measures on the wellbeing of people fail to consider the importance of natural resources. Human development is mostly assessed from an economic perspective by measuring GDP or Gross National

Product (GNP), which are based on income. There are only a few recent indices that attempt to incorporate the value of natural resources into our economy, mainly for the cost of pollution or the value of the loss of natural capital. There are many benefits of ecosystems (e.g. spiritual, cultural) that are important for our wellbeing but are beyond a price tag. Some famous economists such as Herman Daly, Robert Costanza, Partha Dasgupta and others have claimed that we need to include the natural resources as a base for human development (that includes our economy as a part of the system), as shown in Daly's Triangle below (Fig. 4.2):

Daly's Triangle

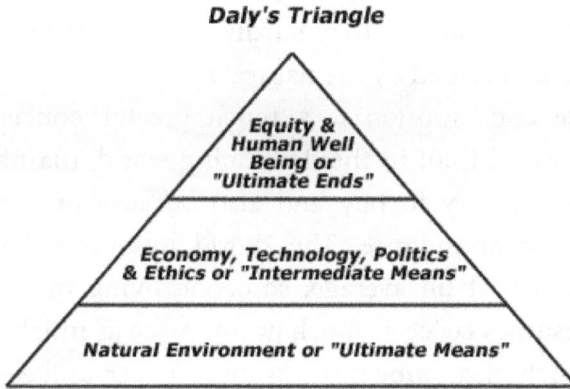

Fig. 4.2.   Daly's Triangle of Sustainability (Daly 1973).

There has been significant progress made over the last few years at the international level to move economies away from conventional GDP measures. As GDP does not provide a full picture of economics, for example, one may be happy with fewer commodities but living closer to nature or for living a peaceful life. Our modern measures of economy fail to reflect such measures. The real meaning of development that includes liberty of human (social and individual) and natural values is often missed. Natural resources are the basis of our development

— socio-cultural, economic as well as our spiritual and emotional development. The irony is that these are often ignored in development measures. A significant challenge is how we can incorporate natural resources into our economic measures that can be used by policy decision-makers to suggest our actual status of development.

The modern western society is based on intensive use of resources, and it is not inappropriate to call our modern society an 'intense resource-use society'. People usually perceive development as access to commodities or to be able to afford an expensive lifestyle. Our modern lifestyle is very resource intensive. Although, societies in the developed world are largely dependent on resources, they hardly realise that most of these resources are provided by the natural systems.

Resource consumption is a much greater concern in the developed world than in the developing world, mainly because of people's capacity to buy and also because of the resource availability or abundance. The World Resources (2000–2001) report stated that on average, someone living in a developed nation consumes twice as much grain, twice as much fish, three times as much meat, nine times as much paper, and eleven times as much gasoline as someone living in a developing nation (Fig. 4.3 and Data Table 4.1 below). Moreover, the consumers in high-income countries — about 16 per cent of the world's population — accounted for 80 per cent of the money spent on private consumption in 1997, i.e. $14.5 trillion of the $18 trillion total (World Resources 2000–2001).

Global Share of Private Consumption, 1997 (in billions)

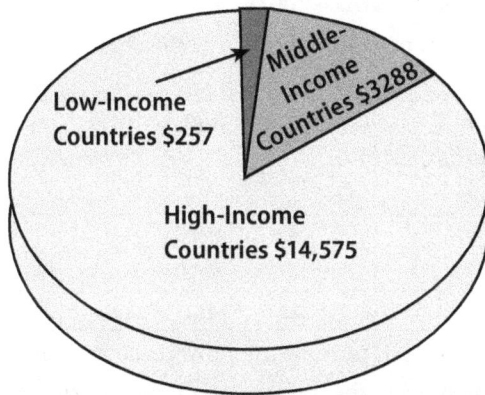

Fig. 4.3:   *Global share of private consumption*
            (source: World Resources 2000–2001)

Table 4.1: Disparities in Consumption: Annual per Capita Consumption in Selected High-, Medium- and Low-Income Nations (source: World Resources 2000–2001)							
	Total Value of	Fish	Meat	Cereals	Paper	Fossil Fuels	Passenger Cars
	Private Consumption*	(kg)	(kg)	(kg)	(kg)	(kg of oil equivalent)	(per 1,000 people)
Country	(1997)	(1997)	(1998)	(1997)	(1998)	(1997)	(1996)
United States	$21,680	21.0	122.0	975.0	293.0	6,902	489.0
Singapore	$16,340	34.0	77.0	159.0	168.0	7,825	120.0
Japan	$15,554	66.0	42.0	334.0	239.0	3,277	373.0
Germany	$15,229	13.0	87.0	496.0	205.0	3,625	500.0
Poland	$5,087	12.0	73.0	696.0	54.0	2,585	209.0
Trinidad/ Tobago	$4,864	12.0	28.0	237.0	41.0	6,394	94.0
Turkey	$4,377	7.2	19.0	502.0	32.0	952	55.0
Indonesia	$1,808	18.0	9.0	311.0	17.0	450	12.2
China	$1,410	26.0	47.0	360.0	30.0	700	3.2
India	$1,166	4.7	4.3	234.0	3.7	268	4.4

	Total Value of	Fish	Meat	Cereals	Paper	Fossil Fuels	Passenger Cars
	Private Consumption*	(kg)	(kg)	(kg)	(kg)	(kg of oil equivalent)	(per 1,000 people)
Bangladesh	$780	11.0	3.4	250.0	1.3	67	0.5
Nigeria	$692	5.8	12.0	228.0	1.9	186	6.7
Zambia	$625	8.2	12.0	144.0	1.6	77	17.0

Table 4.1: Disparities in Consumption: Annual per Capita Consumption in Selected High-, Medium- and Low-Income Nations (source: World Resources 2000–2001)

*Adjusted to reflect actual purchasing power, accounting for currency and cost of living differences (the 'purchasing power parity' approach).

(Details of sources: Total Private Consumption (except China and India): World Bank 1999: Table 4.11; (fish) Laureti 1999: 48–55; (meat) WRI et al. 2000a: Agriculture and Food Electronic Database; (paper) WRI et al. 2000b: DataTable ERC.5; (fossil fuels) WRI et al. 2000b: DataTable ERC.2; (passenger cars) WRI et al. 2000b: DataTable ERC.5).

In becoming resource-use societies in developed countries, people are often at a distance from the raw resources (as discussed in the previous chapter). This further leads to unsustainable development that means we can't develop forever given the current rate of consumption and waste production. To develop sustainable societies, the important main aspects to consider are:

i.   social equity or fair distribution of resources,

ii. allocation of resources in an appropriate and justified way, and

iii. sustainable use of resources.

If there is inclusion of these principles of Ecological Economics in future development related projects, it will certainly reflect sustainable outcomes for human society. In the modern world, there are issues with distribution and allocation, as well as with the use of resources that applies at different levels (individuals, societies or nations). Sustainable scale is a major issue in developed countries while fair distribution and allocation of resources seems to be predominant issues in developing countries.

These three aspects of resource use could be linked to each other depending upon the scale and usage of resources.

There is the unequal distribution of resources among people at a global, national, regional and even at a local scale. Within developing countries sometimes these disparities can be so large that it is hard for us to comprehend the differences between low, medium and high income families. Globally, there are huge differences in the average per capita income in developing and developed countries. This difference affects people's ability to make choices about their resource use, thus affecting the sustainable scale.

Due to the recent global financial crisis in many developing countries, there are increased pressures on people to meet their personal demands for food, shelter and clothes. As a consequence, natural resources often remain ignored even though people use them for their daily living. People's welfare is dependent on the natural resources but, unfortunately, the focus of the current economy for development is usually on commodities and access to facilities, not on the welfare of individuals or societies. The effort to live makes it hard for people to think beyond their immediate needs, and moreover often there are no government policies or effective strategies in place that reflect the natural resources' value. In such circumstances, there is a missing link between people and their use of natural resources. And, there is a need to put effort into emphasising those links, particularly for the main basic demands that are fulfilled from the natural resources. One would imagine that people in developing countries depend highly on natural resources for their prime needs (food/fodder/ medicine etc.), so there should be a greater focus on natural resources to improve people's welfare. Unfortunately, this is often not the situation, mainly due to the failure of our current economic system to incorporate such non-monetary values of natural systems. Since the usual economic tools are applied so the role of natural resources in the livelihoods of poor people are often missed, thus resulting in inappropriate policies.

It is often thought (at a country and individual scale) that those who are economically well-off can think more about saving their environment. Whereas, those who are poor can't spend as much effort thinking about saving their environment as they need to concentrate on access to the basic resources of living. This may be true to some extent and could be the main reason for the exploitation of natural resources in many developing countries.

However, I also think it depends on how we view the economy in the developing and developed world situations. Rich countries often outsource their consumer needs/products, and thus indirectly contribute to consume other's resources (a poor country may serve as a source of those products). In doing so, they outsource some environmental problems that otherwise would have created pollution and/or used on-site resources. There is also a need to account for the on-site as well as off-site environmental pollution and use of resources.

For example, Australia has outsourced the production of many products to China. The Chinese pay the cost of any bad environmental effects from the production of these products. The cost of such externalities for the countries that carry out the production can be environmental degradation, health issues, social issues, etc. If we broaden our thinking to the level of planet Earth as a house, then we need to avoid any products or processes that contribute to environmental degradation anywhere on Earth.

The rich/developed countries, with developed technology, may have reduced the pollution problems to some extent but their level of consumption per capita is certainly very high compared to poor/less developed countries as mentioned earlier. In developing countries, the misuse of natural resources and pollution are major concerns, whereas in developed countries over-use of resources is the major environmental concern. Both

ways, we are losing our precious natural resources on our planet
— a home for all of us!

People in the economically poor countries struggle to fulfill
their basic needs, and often the environment, or natural resources
are targeted as a way of fulfilling their basic needs. Sustainable
resource use is often ignored particularly in the absence of
effective government policies. This is quite a strange situation.
Although poor people may depend upon their surrounding
natural resources more than people in developed countries, they
may actually over-exploit their resources without realising that
they are harming their basic resource on which their livelihoods
depend. Competition for survival or exploitation of common
resources is common worldwide in the absence of effective
policies. The free-rider effect that nature's benefits are freely
available to reap makes people focus on their personal benefits
without realising the depletion costs. Many such examples exist
throughout the world where resources are depleted because of
poor management and lack of policies to regulate resource use.
In developed countries, people usually have access to the natural
resources and governments can afford to save the resources that
are at risk or avoid degradation of those resources.

We cannot generalise human attitudes to say that people
living in a rich country care more for the environment than
those living in a poor country. There will be exceptions in both
places. On one hand, not all people in a developed country
care for the environment, it is rather that most people become
'intensive resource-use' creatures as I discussed earlier. On the
other hand, not all people in a poor country exploit the resources,
as we know many tribal/rural communities manage resources
effectively for their survival. Perhaps, those countries that are in
the middle pathway where economic development has achieved
a certain level so that people have access to basic needs (but not
all the services/facilities as in a developed country) can provide
a better answer to the question of whether people change

their attitude and habits to realise the importance of natural resources once their basic needs are met or not? Or whether people in economically well-off countries actually become more environmentally aware but pollute the environment more by using a greater number of resources? Or as we discussed earlier on the topic of waste recycling, that they develop techniques and capacity to deal with the environmental problems?

It is difficult to correlate that people in developed economies better care for their environment. I think that people in developed economies may be well aware of environmental issues, but become intensive resource-users and lack in application of their environmental knowledge. Compared to this, people in the developing economies have a prime focus on livelihoods and are often limited by their needs. Some kind of eco-measure to include natural resources into development measures can help us to address these issues on resource use, both in the developed and developing countries. I imagine a hybrid economy that includes both monetary as well as non-monetary aspects of our living, or at least those that we value highly in our living.

There has been some progress in the last 10 years or so on developing such measures such as GPI (Gross Progress Indicators) or sustainability measures such as SEEA (System of Environmental Economic Accounts), SNI (Sustainable National Income), ISEW (Index of Sustainable Economic Welfare) etc., but these still have a strong focus on economic welfare with some degree of sustainability components. There is yet a long way to go to develop measures that are away from GDP, which is a macro-economic based tool, to natural resource based tools for measuring development.

Ultimately, whatever way we measure our development, we as individuals and as modern societies need to realise the value of our natural resources in our living. We need to awaken our conscious to lead better lives.

Value assessment of my use of ecosystem services on a daily basis

As mentioned earlier in Chapter 2, I evaluated my daily natural resources use to understand the value of those resources in my life. I roughly calculated the monetary value of some services as follows: a glass of water (AUD 1), tea (AUD 1.50), bread, jam and butter for breakfast (AUD 3), meals at lunch and dinner time (AUD 10) and afternoon tea (AUD 2). So roughly I consume materials worth AUD 17.50 for my survival every day, and all this comes from Mother Nature — of course with human efforts. These are conservative estimates compared to the market prices, and for many people this value could be as high as AUD 40 per day. Let's take a rough average of AUD 20 per day for consuming food items. This amounts to AUD 7300 per person per year using very conservative values only for food items.

However, I have excluded other important services such as air to breath, water for cleansing/drinking, and visits to parks or other natural places for enjoyment. Some of these services are irreplaceable and can't be assigned a price tag. Anyway, let's include the price for water usage (from the municipal/city council charges) that depends upon the area/council one lives in. I include here AUD 700 per year per person for simplicity (which is what I pay as my share in Toowoomba, Queensland). This brings the total value, on average to AUD 8000 per person per year for the tangible services we get from our natural resources.

Then, I can include the value of daily visits to parks and bushland, depending upon my willingness to pay. For example, say AUD 1 per visit means on average if a person visits a park on 300 days per year, the total value is AUD 300 per person per year. And we include here an average cost of about AUD 250 per person per year for visiting the national parks or other natural recreational areas we use for recreation, education and for fishing, etc. The total value of the main services is AUD 8550 per year and this excludes the value of the good air we breathe, the 'assimilation' of waste that we produce and the many educational, cultural, spiritual and identity values we have for our natural systems. There are also other important values such as solitude, health and recreation (children's play) in public gardens. Most importantly, many of the services we get from nature are irreplaceable.

Therefore, the actual value will be beyond the figures I calculated in here. However, these figures do provide some rough estimate of the services that we, most directly, derive from Mother Nature.

In the end, if I tentatively put a rough figure on the services derived from nature, I could easily reach approximately AUD 20,000 per year. When we compare that with what we spend on other 'marketable' items, what we earn, then the intangible values represents a significant proportion of the total budget, but we don't get to realise this benefit for which we pay nothing. We hardly value or understand the importance of nature for providing us these services. Most importantly, many services such as cultural, educational or recreation that we obtain from nature are irreplaceable and can't be bought from the market.

Imagine if we needed to pay or account for all the services we get from nature for our living. There will be another 'Big Bill' that will come from nature, probably the largest of all the bills that we currently pay. Our lives would be very cumbersome with the number of every item we use from Mother Nature and their respective payments. The list of our accounts for borrowing would be too long! This simple exercise suggests how much we already owe to Mother Nature, and it may help us realise the effects of our actions.

The important part of this whole exercise is that we realise and understand the value of benefits that we derive from natural systems. In reality, this value would be much greater than the very conservative estimates suggested here. In our economy, we account for every single dollar we spend on 'marketable' items

— clothes, furniture, car, etc. We make our house budget and plan our expenditures accordingly. However, with nature's services, we do not account for water, air or other materials that are our very basic needs to live. And we rarely think of 'nature' for fulfilling such needs. Most of these services are considered a free gift and nature does not collect debt if we fail to pay. It comes to our moral responsibility that at least for consuming some things from nature, we are responsible to return some things to nature.

Measuring the value of these services is not the aim of this book, rather our main goal is *to realise* the importance of these services in our lives. Dollar values of various items is a man-made tool to deal and manage items in his or her way but if we really want to learn and manage our items as an 'ideal civilised society' then self-realisation is the way to go. Often, we miss learning about ourselves, that is, our inner being or self-realisation. We all know that we will not take anything with us when we die. We are a part of this overall universal system, like all other creatures on Earth. Self-realisation is an important tool for all of us that can help in exploring our connections with Mother Nature and to living our lives in a peaceful way. Certainly, it's the one I'd like for all of us to understand — the role of nature in our living.

My basic economic needs for wellbeing

I am an ecologist, so my first thoughts are that I do not become a burden (ecologically) on our planet. Thus, firstly I will analyse the natural resources that I use or depend upon in my daily life, starting my day in the morning:

1. Water.
2. Natural beauty, serenity and the outlook of parks that I visit in the mornings for regular walks.
3. Food items, cooked and uncooked (unlimited list such as fruits, vegetables, eggs, milk, honey, peanut butter, nuts, cereals, bread etc.).
4. Beverages: tea and coffee (amount two–four cups per day).

5. Petrol to move around, and electricity and gas for day-to-day activities that are generated from natural resources.
6. Waste disposal that nature and/or man-made technology takes care of and helps to process.
7. House (bricks, cement, wood/timber and other household items).
8. Clothes.

I use or get benefits for the above mentioned resources from nature, but I hardly realise this in my day-to-day life and I barely return anything to nature. Probably, this is a common example for many of us. I could do at least a little service to nature as a responsible citizen of Earth by planting some trees in my backyard, or growing some vegetables and herbs to generate my own produce. I also make indirect contributions by promoting sustainable agriculture and related practices, and passing on ecological knowledge and an understanding of natural systems through teaching at university and school.

Above all, my basic necessities are food, shelter and clothes. Almost, all the items in my daily life come from the natural world in a direct and indirect way. However, when we consider my wellbeing as per the standards set by the Australian Bureau of Statistics (ABS) then it will be estimated from my income, housing, education, time for leisure and family etc. (ABS 2001). There is no mention of the many intangible services/benefits that I derive from the natural systems, or of how I value the natural world around me and how much I depend upon it for my living or how well I feel being in contact with nature. So the non-financial part of nature that I consider valuable for my wellbeing remains largely unaccounted for. Although in a real sense, many aspects of my wellbeing are derived from nature and are a part of my household micro-economy.

Another aspect of my wellbeing that is also worth considering is that many of the items, such as food, clothes, a house, furniture, car, petrol etc. I am able to afford only if I am earning a reasonable income. This is a measureable aspect that is well reflected in the modern economy and can help to categorise whether I am living well or poorly. No doubt that this measurable of economy (having some security for living, food etc.) helps me to think about the environment and to do my best to live in harmony with nature. This is certainly an advantage for living in the developed world (recall our earlier discussion on developing *vs.* developed countries), however, it does not completely reflect our well-being.

This measureable side of the economy is a main interest for many of us, i.e. to work/earn money to afford the items that we need to live, and this is predominantly used to reflect our wellbeing (without accounting the non-marketable nature related values). In Australia, the basic income starts from approximately AUD 400 per week as the minimum. Let's take the example of AUD 400 per week, I claim that this is sufficient amount to live a happy, healthy and contented life if one wants to and is skilled to manage funds in the right way. Although, it is just enough to survive and there is limited saving ability. For families with kids, it is a different situation. I believe that if we know how to live a happy and healthy life, we can survive well in our currently available resources. It is about building the capacity to survive in whatever is available and to strive for hard work that helps us to live a balanced life. Unfortunately, the non-marketable side of our wellbeing (which mostly relates to nature) is such an important aspect of human life and has been largely overlooked in our formal ways of education.

Role of natural resources in the modern economy: the 'invisible backbone': development *vs.* wellbeing

We have been discussing development and wellbeing in last few sections. But, what is the difference between these two? Development broadly means developing choices or utilities for people so people are able to afford items that they may like. Whereas, wellbeing mostly means 'feeling well' being satisfied with what you have or want to have. So, the two concepts vary in their meaning from an economic perspective. Noble Laureate, Prof. Amartya Sen has nicely framed 'development' as freedom for enabling people to lead a creative and healthy life; integrating the concepts of development and wellbeing (Sen 1985, 1993, 1999 a and b). However, there is yet a demarcation in the economic discipline about how we perceive development or wellbeing. Since our focus is on a conventional view of development 'increasing utility', so the current economy mainly focuses on commodities/ materials that enhance development (as evident from wellbeing measures applied by the ABS (2001).

In the current economic global crisis, the world economies are going through a difficult situation where on one side we are encountering the failures of market economies, while at the same time we are starting to realise the impact of climate change and of other environmental effects on our living. Climatic events such as floods, cyclones, tornados and bush fires are becoming more and more common (State of Climate 2012 and 2014). The positive side of these two coinciding difficulties is that it provides us with an opportunity for a new way of thinking that can help sustain human livelihoods.

In Australia, our current economy is based on the ideology of unlimited economic growth, as evident from the focus of current government policies on mining and marketable sectors of the economy. This is based upon the conventional belief that increasing utility will enhance Australians' wellbeing. This is what we mostly mean when we talk about 'development'.

However, the correlation between human wellbeing and 'development', as commonly perceived by people, is no longer true. We need to identify what went wrong in the equation of development as a means to enhance human wellbeing. Development is not at all related to maximising the benefits from the materialistic items or having the most comfortable items in life. As Sen (1993, 1999a and b) points out that development is much beyond that. It is about the capability of people to lead the lives they want to lead. Often, we forget this real meaning of development and limit our thinking to materialistic achievements!

When we come out of this conventional notion of development, there are many aspects of our development that play a crucial role in our wellbeing, such as being satisfied with life or leading a creative and healthy life. These aspects are directly and indirectly related to natural systems, i.e. the natural capital plays a significant role in our development.

It has been argued by Daly (1996) in his book *Beyond Growth — The Economics of Sustainable Development* that to achieve sustainable development, we must consider natural resources. He suggested that our economy is a subset of global ecosystems, and it cannot grow forever. For development, the bottom line is claimed to be built by natural and social capital. In the past, natural and social capitals were abundant, so the market economy progressed without any limitations. However, the scenario is different now where natural capital is limited and declining (as reported by many scientists across the globe and particularly, the recent MA reports in 2005). We have generally accounted for the built and social capital (to some extent) for development, but rarely the natural capital.

There is a need to bring a change in our notion of 'development'. We need to consider the holistic perspective of human wellbeing that is in harmony with nature and applies the main principles for fair distribution, allocation and sustainable use of resources. Our standards for development also need to measure natural wealth. These should not focus only on possession of materials/utility or the capacity to earn to afford those materials, but also on the natural wealth. The present concept of development requires a re-structuring in applying the basic concept of human wellbeing as feeling the very best for every human being on Earth. Its aim should be to enable individuals to lead the life that they want to live in contrast to a utility-oriented wellbeing. In the modern economy, are we achieving this? No.

For the sake of development, which is mostly economy focused, we are losing our social and natural capital. We have moved away from the idea that most of our development today is because of our natural wealth. A simple way to realise the role of natural wealth in our development is to seek our 'connections' to the natural resources. I attempted to highlight these connections between natural capital and human needs in this book, which are otherwise quite often hidden from economic perspectives, simply for the fact that we do not account for the natural capital, and/or we think that items come from the industry that isolates us from the raw materials.

Our natural resources underpin our economy and have become a limiting factor. Among the main components of development — social, environment and economics — if one is not functional, the others cannot function well. We have just started to feel the impacts of failure of any one system. At present, the environmental/natural sector limits our 'development' as the natural resources are becoming more and more limiting. The law of limiting factors in the current economic theory has failed to recognise this 'natural' component mainly because of the absence of price tags and lack of policies that account for the natural resources. Without realising and improving the status of our natural resources, it will be difficult for us to 'develop', that is, to enhance the wellbeing of people any further.

Ecological economics:

This is a new discipline that emerged out of economics and ecology in 1980s. This discipline builds upon integrating the two disciplines of economics and ecology as:
- *Eco-nomics*: management of the household (people's household).
- *Ecology*: study of the household (nature's household).
  (Costanza and Daly 1987)

The 'Ecological Economics' discipline aims to analyse and understand the relationships between ecosystems and economics. It is a trans-disciplinary field that crosses the boundaries of economics, ecology and social sciences. It is about making economics more cognizant of ecological impacts, systems and human dependencies. And it is easier to understand from a household perspective as it includes many non-marketable values that we have been discussing earlier.

There has been significant progress in the last 20–30 years to advance thinking of economy for incorporating ecological perspectives. Costanza et al. (1997) published a famous article in *Nature* on the value of world's ecosystem services that assessed the monetary value of world's major ecosystem services as USD 33 trillion per year. Daily (1997) highlighted the people's dependence on natural ecosystems in his book on natures' services.

In the last 10–20 years, several European economies have shifted their focus from industrial economy to nature-based economy or to maintain natural wealth. Many have attempted to assess their natural resources by understanding the links of ecosystem services with people's wellbeing (the Sub-global Assessment Network reports many such case studies conducted in various parts of Europe at www.ecosystemassessments.net).

A 'change' in thinking

Natural resources are the 'backbone' in any economy and play a direct and/or indirect role to support the kind of progress we want to achieve. This 'invisible' role of natural resources cannot be overlooked any longer for two reasons:

1. Degrading ecosystems due to over-exploitation for human use leads to fewer ecosystem goods and services (MA 2005).
2. Climate change will have severe consequences for people's livelihoods (MA 2005).

We need to reshape our economy in a way that helps us realise the importance of natural resources for our livelihoods, which may be eco-economy or green economy. For this, we need to develop a new concept for 'development'. A concept that allows 'people to lead lives that they have reason to value' (Sen 1999), with a focus on improving wellbeing while recognising the provision of basic services (food/medicine, air, water, clothes, shelter, education and health) for livelihood. This would require connectivity to natural resources and development in terms of being 'well', not just increasing utility. We need to ask ourselves the following fundamental questions: 1. What are the prime needs for our living? 2. How are these needs fulfilled? 3. How can we sustain the resources that provide us with those services at an individual, community, regional or global scale?

For this new concept of development, we need to change our current consumer levels especially in the developed world, and subsequently the measures to assess development and wellbeing of humans, so that we move away from 'utility'. To enhance wellbeing, we need to build a new model of economy that:

1. sustains the use of natural resources,
2. enhances human capabilities,
3. maximises the social capital, and
4. provides opportunities to lead the lives that we want.

There are several other socio-economic factors that can help to enhance our wellbeing depending upon culture, natural systems and geography. However, the natural systems are of prime importance and are critical for our wellbeing. We need to incorporate ecological value of resources and the access and availability of these resources as vital components of our wellbeing. Basically, there is a need to change our thinking from predominantly maximising benefits to sustenance of livelihoods, from consumerism to 'self-contended' and 'self-sufficiency' by generating and sustaining food and other much needed basic materials for living, and by processing the waste/re-using the waste that we produce to some extent, at an every individual's scale.

Steady-state economy:

I would like to mention the concept of a 'steady-state economy' that was introduced by Daly in the 1970s. This concept is still prevalent and many ecological economists are still arguing to consider economy to be a sub-part of the environment.

Daly (1970s, 1991, 1992, 1996, 2005 and 2013 and Costanza et al. 1987, 2007, 2014) argued in favour of a steady economy and remained critical of how big (physical scale or size of human presence in the ecosystem) the economy can become given that overall economy is a subset of the natural environment. Daly advocated that man-made economy is a 'subset' of the environment and that there are limits to the man-made economy's growth (Fig. 4.4).

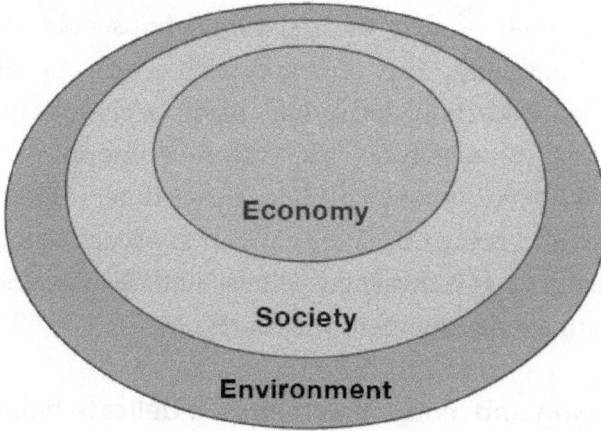

Fig. 4.4:   *Economy as a subset of environment as suggested by Daly (1977).*

This is proving true now when we are realising our dependence on natural resources and experiencing the impacts of climate change. Another convincing argument put forth by Boulding in 1966 was about moving from a 'cowboy economy' to a 'spaceship Earth'. He argues that we must move away from an economy where we perceive our resources as unlimited. He argued that our planet Earth is like a 'spaceship' with limited resources and with a circular flow of resources — some acting as a source and some as a sink. He suggested the main three spaceship Earth functions are to supply resources (renewable and non-renewable), to assimilate waste products and to provide humans with natural services such as aesthetic enjoyment, recreation and spiritual fulfillment. These main functions are regarded as functions of life support. There are limits to our Earth spaceship.

A new approach is needed to bring a change in our thinking to say 'it's enough for me' and to consider ourselves as a part of Mother Nature, not as the superior beings to any other living organisms on Earth. This will lead to us realising our dependence upon natural resources and ultimately, it will help us to achieve the actual goal of 'eco-nomy', that is, management of our household — first the individual household and then the global household. This new approach when applied at an individual or household level, will bring a change in micro-economy and ultimately in our macro-economy. Then our worldview for development will change over time. I am sure once we, as the public, bring this change in our approach to looking at development, the governmental policies will change, and hence our new path for development will start!

Our wellbeing and material demands: a delicate balance

Ultimately, economics is all about managing the household and making choices. There are many ways for people to be satisfied from a materials perspective. However, my question is: does that really make us happy?

For many people, the answer may be 'yes' in the initial and mid-years of our lives, but towards the mid-end of our life's spectrum or once we approach the middle age and have the materials that we wanted, we realise that ultimately it is our self-satisfaction/contentedness/happiness that is the most important. The resources and materials are important to live our lives comfortably; however, these are not the only ways/means to make us happy or contented. If the materials were the only thing that made people happy, then people living in the richer countries would be much happier compared to people living in the developing countries. But that is not true.

The United Nations reports on happiness suggest that people living in countries such as Bhutan are happier than many others in this world. Bhutan has rich natural resources and people respect and value their resources from cultural, educational, spiritual and identity perspectives. We'll discuss this in detail in the next chapter.

The great sages, such as Buddha and others, have taught humanity, time and again, that material gain alone will not fulfill our deepest needs. Material life must be harnessed to meet the human needs, most importantly to promote the end of suffering, social justice, freedom and to attain happiness. This challenge — to promote the end of the suffering, social justice and the attainment of happiness — is real for all of us living in different parts of the world (World Happiness Report by Helliwell et al. 2012). One example is the US, which has achieved economic and technological progress over the last 50 years without much gain in self-reported happiness of its citizens. This suggests that there must be some other reasons, other than just the materials for economic progress (World Happiness Report 2012).

I believe self-satisfaction will play an important role in making us a less resource-use society as well as to leading us onto a sustainable path of living, which will ultimately lead to our wellbeing. If self-satisfaction is the main goal in our lives then how can we achieve that?

We all will have different answers for this. However, the main aspect is to explore our inner being to actually know what we really want and to work out the ways to achieve what we want, but in a sustainable and logical way. I wonder if this is something we face every day yet we mostly ignore and keep on running towards material wealth. We do not want to think from a long-term perspective or to know what exactly we want in our life. We lack the capabilities and skills to explore our inner-self and to work out how to live life in a 'right' way from the beginning. This important lesson is largely missing in our learnings at schools and universities. There is a need to educate people to analyse their needs, introspect their desires, and to suit their desires with nature, wherever possible. There is a need to develop balance between what we want and how much we should have, particularly where economic affordability is not an issue. We need to apply the principle 'this is sufficient for me' if we really want to sustain our wellbeing.

When I think, superficially, about what I really want, my vague answer is to have some material resources that includes:

- a small house (possibly environmentally-friendly) that is at walking distance to a workplace and school,
- a backyard where I can grow herbs, vegetables and fruits,
- some household comforts,
- a stable and secure social environment,
- a safe and clean natural environment,
- freedom to lead a creative and healthy life, and
- availability and access to natural places such as parks or bush areas or recreational areas.

Indeed, what I really want is some spiritual space and the opportunity to work and live a peaceful life. To exactly know what I want and how can I achieve it, I need to develop my capabilities that enable me to achieve my goals. How much I can achieve out of the listed items will actually depend upon my efforts and the choices and opportunities that I make or get, and these may vary with time and circumstances. This is where my self-analysis and introspection helps me to redefine my needs and to constantly remind me of the main goal of life — living peacefully. For me, this peaceful living will not be possible without having a closeness with nature that includes a spiritual component. Through meditation and yoga, my inner being helps to remind me of my ultimate goal. I didn't get this knowledge to understand myself through schools or universities; I would have perceived it in parts while observing other people, family members and through personal experiences. This learning greatly helped me to constantly analyse my inner-self. Mostly, due to the busy routine in the modern world, we fail to learn from our peers/parents/grandparents or other family members. As a result, most of us just learn as we grow and quite often it takes us a lifetime. In our seventies, we realise that we have collected more than what was needed, then we wish we would have known a few things earlier.

To know what we want should be the main task in our lives, and we need to get the time to explore our own thinking right from the very beginning. Exploring our desires can lead us to live the life we want to live and will help us to define our economy at a household scale, which will then have a local and regional impact.

A simple example is that we can start working on the household economy right from our own household by growing vegetables/fruits, etc. Economics at a household level applies the same principles as at a macro-economy level, except that the scale is small. Some items could be difficult to comprehend in terms of dollar values, as there may not be any market/price tag. For example, growing vegetables and fruits will contribute to the household economy through multiple benefits, such as saving the cost of vegetables if bought from the markets, contributing to good health or to emotional wellbeing. But these are largely valuable for our household economy. Moreover, there are social benefits from sharing the produce and sharing knowledge that are also beyond the normal economic techniques/methods for measurements. This 'error' in measurements will have an impact on the micro-economy for not reflecting the actual value of our micro-economy (and can actually project a decline). In a true sense, this kind of economy will improve our household savings. If all the people in a town did so, it would have a great impact on the market economy for that town. Therefore, our household economy can be a starting point to bring a change in the macro-economy.

The main flow-on economic benefits from household produce to the household economy include:

- Chemical free home-grown vegetables and fruits (cost saving as well as health benefits);
- Health benefits from working in the gardens and for eating healthy food;
- Enhancement of knowledge;
- Networking and social cohesion among the society;
- Enhancement of learning skills for children;
- Reducing the use of in-house electrical equipment (such as the TV/computer) when one is working outside in the garden;
- Improving the environment for growing trees and vegetables that will produce oxygen, and will consume (sequester) carbon dioxide from the atmosphere;
- Enhancing aesthetic beauty.

Gardening to grow vegetables and fruits is one example, there are many others that you can explore to improve your household economy.

Overall for a household, we do need to work and earn enough to meet all the expenses such as to pay bills, council rates, house rent or repayments, etc. So we are a part of a micro- and a macro-economy, but we need a balance. No doubt that economics in terms of our earning capacity plays a significant part in our lives. However, we also need to consider many other aspects of our lives that are important to enhance our wellbeing. And these other aspects of life usually come next, once we are able to earn enough to support ourselves financially. I believe that we are able to afford our basic living, so our wellbeing should be of paramount importance for us to lead healthy and creative lives. The various aspects of wellbeing which are quite important to make our lives satisfactory, are actually the values embedded in our living that we all care about, such as:

- happiness,
- access to good air and water,
- security,
- social relations,
- health and spiritual living,
- freedom to do things that we like to do, and
- cultural and other recreational activities.

These all are the important constituents of our wellbeing, however, the degree of their importance will vary from person to person, but they do play a significant role in everyone's life. In the developed countries, we do not face the same burden of economic insecurity as people in developing countries, but still we lack on many of these above-mentioned aspects of wellbeing in our society. Compared to this, in the developing world, people do not have that many opportunities to earn enough for basic living but still, they generally tend to be contented with what they have. What are the reasons behind these differences? Some of these are discussed in the next chapter and some I leave for you to explore.

In conclusion, this chapter attempts to connect our household economy (from a micro-, and macro-economy scale) with our daily wellbeing while raising awareness of our resource use, applying practises that sustain the use of natural resources and helping us to realise our dependence on natural resources. We discussed the concept of human development and wellbeing with a vision that our future economies focus on people's wellbeing to enable them to lead creative and healthy lives. This chapter re-enforces the idea of the importance of nature's connections that are paramount to enhance our wellbeing.

5

Social world

*'A certain degree of physical harmony and comfort is
necessary, but above a certain level it becomes a hindrance
instead of a help. Therefore, the ideal of creating an
unlimited number of wants and satisfying them seems to
be a delusion and a snare.'*

— Mahatma Gandhi

It is a fact that all the people in the developed world are not
that happy, although there are plenty of resources and services
available. The World Happiness report by Helliwell et al. (2012)
highlights that the realities of poverty, anxiety, environmental
degradation and unhappiness in the midst of great plenty should
not be regarded as mere curiosities. They require our urgent
attention and especially so at this juncture in human history.
We have entered a new world phase, termed the 'Anthropocene'
by the world's Earth system scientists. The Anthropocene is a
newly invented term that combines two Greek roots: 'anthropo',
which means 'human', and 'cene', which means 'new', as in a new
geological epoch. The Anthropocene is the new epoch in which
humanity, through its technological prowess and population of
7 billion, has become the major driver of changes in the Earth's
physical systems, including the climate, the carbon cycle, the
water cycle, the nitrogen cycle and biodiversity. In a way, the
world has become dominated by humans!

The World Happiness (2012) report suggests the Anthropocene will necessarily reshape our societies. If we continue mindlessly along the current economic trajectory, we risk undermining the Earth's life support systems: food supplies, clean water and a stable climate, which are necessary for human health, and even survival. In years or decades, the conditions of life may become dire in several fragile world regions. We are already experiencing that deterioration of life support systems in the dry lands of the Horn of Africa and parts of Central Asia.

One vital part of the World Happiness (2012) report is that it clearly highlights our dependence on natural resources to survive, but, unfortunately, this is not accounted towards wellbeing or development purposes. In fact, there is no measure available, so far, that integrates natural resources and human wellbeing.

The United Nations Development Programme releases human development reports (HDR) every year that mainly account for three main aspects of human living: life expectancy, income and literacy (HDR 1990, 2009, 2010, 2011, 2013 are a few to mention in here). These HDR reports compare development of people in different regions of the world. In the 2013 report, Norway was ranked in first place, Australia in second place, followed by the Netherlands, which was ranked third, the United States, which was ranked fourth and others. These findings suggest that Australia is doing well in terms of human development in the areas of education, income and health. However, these reports do not encompass the concept of human wellbeing in a real sense for not including the role of natural resources, without which human beings have no chance of being well.

I believe that human wellbeing includes various social, economic and ecological dimensions that matter for people, not just the main socio-economic aspects such as income or health. We have discussed earlier how natural systems play a critical role in our emotional, spiritual, health and physical wellbeing through the provision of various services. Not much research has been done on how to assess human wellbeing as it relates to nature. Until recently, the natural resources that we need to survive have been readily available and are not accounted. For this reason, we commonly measure human wellbeing in terms of our social and financial wealth, not in terms of our relationship to nature.

What does 'wellbeing' really mean?

Wellbeing

Wellbeing literally means living happily or leading a satisfying life. For the common man, wellbeing means feeling well (which encompasses various socio-economic-cultural aspects).

Let's explore from an academic perspective how our wellbeing is measured. The Australian Bureau of Statistics (ABS 2001) defines wellbeing as 'a state of health or sufficiency in all aspects of life'. The subject of wellbeing has been widely researched by many different organisations with various approaches (MA 2003). For this reason, there are varying ideas and definitions of what wellbeing actually means (Alkire 2002 a and b). The Organisation for Economic Co-operation and Development (OECD) states that there is no single definition of human wellbeing because the term includes several facets with complex interactions and the respective importance of each aspect is difficult to identify (2011). Despite this, there is a basic agreement that 'wellbeing' includes the satisfaction of material needs, the experience of freedom, health, personal security, good social relations and a healthy natural environment (Sen 1993 and 1999).

There are three main approaches to wellbeing, according to Diener and Suh (1997):

1. The Economics approach considers that people select things and activities that enhance their utility within the constraints of resources they possess (utilitarianism). This

approach is based upon levels of satisfaction that a person achieves from consuming a good/service. Thus, it is linked to income and utility.

2. The Sociological (normative ideal) approach is based on cultural, religious, philosophical or other norms and ideals considered important for wellbeing. For this, optimal levels of health, income and other economic resources are determined, and wellbeing is measured relative to those reference points.

3. The Behaviour/Psychological (subjective experience) approach believes that different people have different value systems, so personal characteristics determine the type of attributes important to people. Hence, the values of wellbeing will be different for different people.

The utility/economic related approaches are more commonly applied to measure human wellbeing so far. There is no doubt that higher income levels help people to have good access to materials, sanitation, water and food. As income improves from very low levels, human wellbeing also improves. This is true for almost every human being. We need to fulfill the basic needs first, so improvements in income help people to live a safe and secure life. In societies where income levels are already high or, in other words, where there is low marginal utility of income, we expect higher levels of self-satisfaction. But, it is not true in many situations. In developed countries such as Australia where income levels are high and people can meet their basic needs, still they lack personal satisfaction, in general. We expect that if income is critical for people to be content, then once the required income is available, people should be satisfied with their lives, but this is not true. This suggests there must be other reasons we need to consider if we want to reflect people's wellbeing.

In fact, in the developed societies affluence affects people's attitudes and values. People create their own set of traps for materialistic achievements, and once a person is trapped in materials it is very difficult to come out. Richard Easterlin mentioned in the World Happiness (2012; pg. 66) report that if countries grow in income, they become no happier. To understand this relationship, he referred to 37 countries with a long enough range of data (21 years for developed countries, 15 for developing countries and 12 for transitional countries). He found a flat or negative relation between changes in life satisfaction and income per head in each group. This is also true if we introspect ourselves; we may not be happy at all the times when we had higher levels of income. I project a similar hypothetical relationship for Income vs. Self-satisfaction as below (Fig. 5.1):

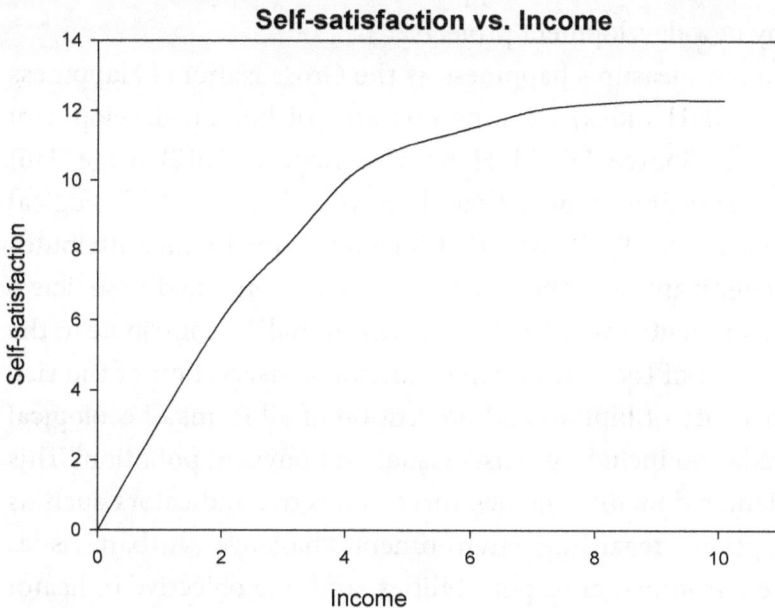

Self-satisfaction vs. Income

Fig. 5.1:   A hypothetical projected relationship between income and level of self-satisfaction of people.

There is a strong message that money or materials are not everything we need in our lives. Apart from the basic household income, there are many other aspects of human living that account for self-satisfaction/happiness such as societal and individual values, cooperation, community trust, physical and mental health, the equality of governance and rule of law from social perspectives, and access and availability of many cultural, identity and spiritual values from ecological-social perspectives. With experience, we learn that upholding our values and rights becomes more important than other things in life.

We'll examine Bhutan as a case study. Bhutan is a developing country but ranks high on happiness indices as highlighted by the World Happiness (2012) report. Since 1972, the King of Bhutan preferred to choose the goals of happiness over wealth and it became an organised principle for governance and policy making to keep people's happiness and wellbeing at the forefront of any new development projects.

Bhutan measures happiness as the Gross National Happiness Index (GNH index) for nine domains of human development (Fig. 5.2; Source World Happiness Report (2012), page 116). It is interesting to note that there is a domain of 'Ecological Diversity' and 'Resilience' that includes some further attributes. It is cognizant with their constitution as mentioned in article 5 (Environment), every Bhutanese citizen shall '…contribute to the protection of the natural environment, conservation of the rich biodiversity of Bhutan and prevention of all forms of ecological degradation including noise, visual and physical pollution'. This particular domain includes three subjective indicators such as perceptions regarding environment challenges, urban issues and environmental responsibilities, and one objective indicator of wildlife damage to crops. For example, the environmental responsibility indicator measures the feelings of personal responsibility to protect the environment, including eco-friendly approaches people apply and knowledge of natural systems. Similarly, spirituality is incorporated into the GNH index under 'psychological wellbeing' as a domain for human development.

The various aspects of the Bhutanese GNH index represent the diverse aspects of human life and could be applied to reflect human development. They are also well beyond the usual socio-economic wellbeing measures we apply here in Australia.

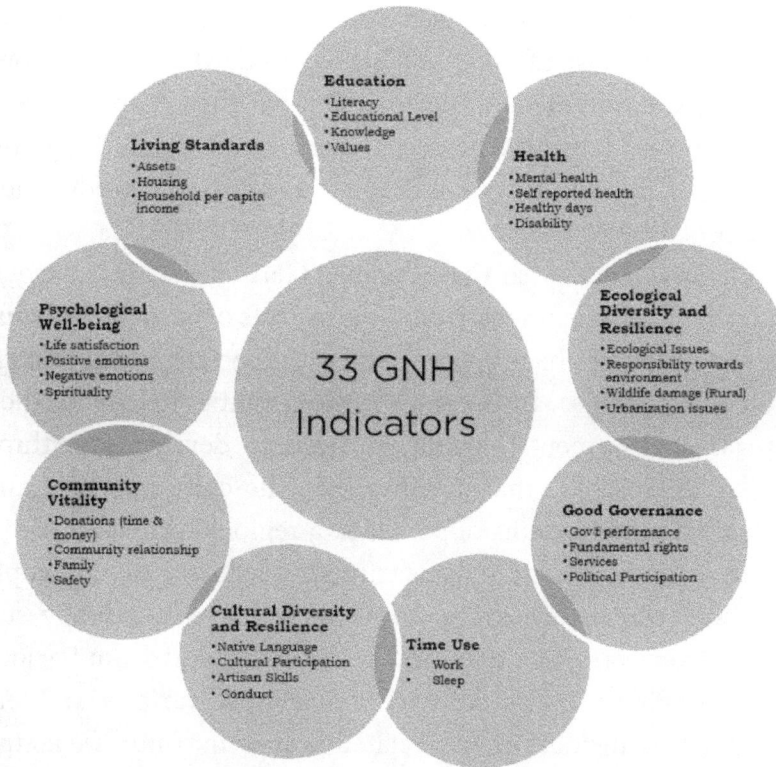

Education
• Literacy
• Educational Level
• Knowledge
• Values

Living Standards
• Assets
• Housing
• Household per capita income

Health
• Mental health
• Self reported health
• Healthy days
• Disability

Psychological Well-being
• Life satisfaction
• Positive emotions
• Negative emotions
• Spirituality

33 GNH Indicators

Ecological Diversity and Resilience
• Ecological Issues
• Responsibility towards environment
• Wildlife damage (Rural)
• Urbanization issues

Community Vitality
• Donations (time & money)
• Community relationship
• Family
• Safety

Good Governance
• Gov't performance
• Fundamental rights
• Services
• Political Participation

Cultural Diversity and Resilience
• Native Language
• Cultural Participation
• Artisan Skills
• Conduct

Time Use
• Work
• Sleep

Fig. 5.2:   The nine domains and 33 indicators of the GNH of Bhutan (Source: World Happiness 2012 report.)

The 'Spirituality' domain (under 'Psychological Wellbeing') in the Bhutanese GNH index is of particular interest for me and makes me think more holistically about our overall wellbeing in life. Spirituality helps us to realise the long-term perspectives. It's not about any faith. It's about being with oneself, being what we are, and exploring our inner-self. The role of the natural environment in spirituality is vital and irreplaceable. If spirituality plays an important role in the wellbeing of humans, then the presence of a natural environment is crucial to providing this service for spirituality. For many tribal societies across the world, spirituality in relation to nature is an important part of their lives.

If we view the whole spectrum of our life, including our spiritual values, we can realise what we need, what we did wrong or right, and how we can improve. But we often do not explore our inner mind due to a perceived lack of time. Regretfully, this training is missing in our schooling and university education system.

I am fascinated with the Bhutanse GNH index. It is a novel concept, which encompasses various aspects of human wellbeing such as education, health, governance, the social system, ecology and cultural values, and people's responsibilities to care for their natural environment. I think we need to develop something similar in Australia that matches with the cultural, social and ecological value systems of people at a regional or local scale. If we are really interested in measuring the wellbeing of our people, then we need to develop a framework that will actually suit people from various urban and rural areas, and from various backgrounds including cultural and identity variations. There is a need to include nature related values into our wellbeing. This kind of framework will help to develop the right policies for future decision-making in relation to human wellbeing or human development. We cannot use an old socio-economic approach that fails to incorporate our values about natural systems. The present ABS wellbeing framework does not suit many, particularly the Indigenous Australian population that has such strong connections with their country/land.

A socio-economic-ecological kind of framework and related measurements will help us to move away from the usual socio-economic concept of wellbeing or the materialistic values towards a new concept of wellbeing where the natural values and/non-materialistic values are considered. Integrating nature's values with our wellbeing to appropriately measure human wellbeing is yet to be achieved.

It is important that we realise we have a limited existence on this planet while valuing the connections we have with our natural surroundings.

Ends and means

I like the concept of the 'ends and means' from a human life perspective, as proposed by Daly and Farley (2004). Ultimately, we all live our lives and work to make the two ends meet together. The ultimate means and the ultimate ends are the two extremes of the ends-means spectrum, as shown below (Fig. 5.3):

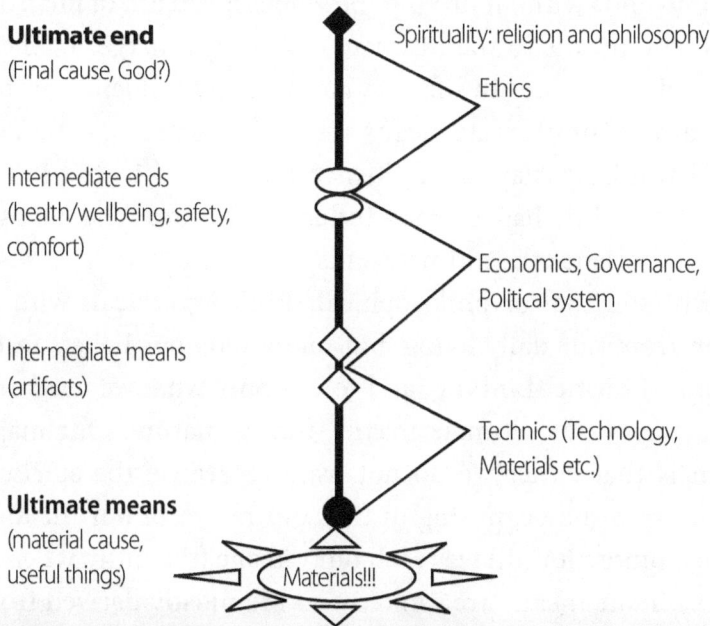

Fig. 5.3: *The ends and means spectrum (adapted from Daly and Farley 2004) that is equivalent to the life line of a person.*

In essence, ultimate human concern should be to use ultimate means efficiently and wisely in the service of the ultimate end. However, this is possible only when we all realise that we have a certain limited amount of ultimate means, and we have to share those resources with each other. Ultimate means also includes natural resources from which we derive a range of ecosystem services as intermediate means (artifacts, food, clothes, shelter etc.). These further lead to meeting our intermediate ends, that is, human wellbeing (for many this means cultural, identity, spiritual and educational values) and that links further to the ultimate end. If we suppose this line of ultimate means and ends represents the 'life line' of a human being, it is easy to understand how the material means and ends flow with the influence of technology and human needs for materials, governance, politics, ethics and spiritual thoughts. In everyday life, we focus on intermediate means and ends without linking the whole spectrum of life from the ultimate means to the ultimate end. It is a merger of these various spheres/values in life that has a strong influence on the continuum of our ultimate means and ends spectrum. Although spiritual thinking may not influence our means in the initial phases, it certainly has a strong influence (towards the old age) once we experience the ultimate ends.

Usually, spiritual or philosophical thinking is dealt with in isolation from our daily living, but many religious beliefs teach us to apply holistic thinking, and to use only what we need and to take care of our ultimate means, that is, nature. Our major problem is that either we do not want to realise the spiritual thinking from the beginning in the continuum of our life and/ or we just ignore it until we reach our old age (the ultimate end).

Our ultimate means are limited and are mostly derived from 'Mother Nature' either directly or indirectly. In response, many religious beliefs suggest that we treat nature as a 'mother'. If we think about tribal communities, they have a much more holistic perspective of thinking than we as the 'educated' citizens of the modern society. I heard a talk by a tribal elder in South Africa where he mentioned the planet Earth as a common place for all humanity. He referred to 'our planet Earth' not just his tribal land or resources. It was amazing to hear that wider perspective about Mother Nature, which we in 'modern' society often lack. We need to apply a similar perspective for our one common house — Earth.

Similarly, Indigenous Australians treat land as a 'mother' and link their physical, spiritual and human worlds well to land. In meetings I have had with traditional Indigenous Australians, their first feelings are always about the country, in that it is 'looking good' or 'looking bad'. If the country is 'looking bad' the people feel sad about it. It's an instant feeling that comes out of considering land, flora and fauna. When I compare that thinking to a scientist such as myself who reports on ecological research, he or she usually reports the status of ecosystems/ nature in isolation from himself/herself, and we often miss integrating and considering ourselves as a part of the system. I think many scientists do not apply the holistic perspective of human connections with the natural world, as we aim to focus on one particular area to research in depth on that very aspect which indirectly keeps us away from the broader perspective that many Indigenous communities possess. Realisation should be an important part of learning in modern societies, whether someone is a scientist or a layperson.

World religions and nature

I highlight here some sayings from various religions on nature (some from an organisation on alliance for religions and conservation, at the website www.arcworld.org).

Buddhism

In general, one is not allowed to kill any fauna because these are all part of the greater life cycle and contribute to nature in their own way.

The relationship between Buddhist ideals and nature contains three contexts:

1. Nature as teacher.
2. Nature as a spiritual force.
3. Nature as a way of life.

The Dalai Lama said, 'A wider more altruistic attitude is very relevant in today's world. If we look at the situation from various angles, such as the complexity and inter-connectedness of the nature of modern existence, then we will gradually notice a change in our outlook, so that when we say "others" and when we think of others, we will no longer dismiss them as something that is irrelevant to us. We will no longer feel indifferent.'

Another quote by the Dalai Lama is, 'Because we all share this planet Earth, we have to learn to live in harmony and peace with each other and with nature. This is not just a dream, but a necessity'. This quote suggests to us the urgency to act to protect not just nature for itself but also because it is critical for our living.

In the words of Maha Ghosananda (a Cambodian Buddhist monk), 'When we respect the environment, then nature will be good to us. When our hearts are good, then the sky will be good to us. The trees are like our mother and father, they feed us, nourish us, and provide us with everything; the fruit, leaves, the branches, the trunk. They give us food and satisfy many of our needs. So we spread the Dharma (truth) of protecting ourselves and protecting our environment, which is the Dharma of the Buddha. When we accept that we are part of a great human family — that every being has the nature of Buddha — then we will sit, talk, make peace. I pray that this realisation will spread throughout our troubled world and bring humankind and the Earth to its fullest flowering. I pray that all of us will realise peace in this lifetime and save all beings from suffering.'

In reality, we should be thinking of ourselves as a part of nature. Unfortunately, with modernisation, our greed has made us exploit the natural resources to maximise our benefits. We treat ourselves as a superpower that controls other living things on this planet and as a separate 'supreme' entity we dominate or possess control over nature. We need to move away from this concept of 'supremacy' and should learn to consider ourselves as a part of nature that has millions of other organisms.

Christianity

These Christian quotes suggest that there is a lot for us to learn from Mother Nature and that some of the values, such as spirituality, cannot be replaced.

- 'The heavens declare the glory of God; the skies proclaim the work of his hands. Day after day they pour forth speech; night after night they display knowledge. There is no speech language where their voice is not heard. Their voice goes out into all the Earth, their words to the ends of the world.' — *Psalm 19:1–4.*
- 'The gravity of the ecological situation reveals how deep is the human moral crisis.' — Pope John Paul II, message for World Peace Day in 1990.
- 'Therefore the land mourns, and all who live in it languish; together with the wild animals and the birds of the air, even the fish of the sea are perishing.' — *Hosea 4:2–3* (cited by Pope John Paul II to back his belief that Earth suffers when humanity turns its back on Creation).
- 'The Lord God took the man and settled him in the Garden

of Eden to cultivate and take care of it.' — *Genesis 2:15*; suggesting humanity's role as stewards of nature, not its masters.

'We need to find God, and he cannot be found in noise and restlessness. God is the friend of silence. See how nature — trees, flowers, grass — grows in silence; see the stars, the moon and the sun, how they move in silence … We need silence to be able to touch souls.'
— Mother Teresa

Hinduism

'Supreme Lord, let there be peace in the sky and in the atmosphere. Let there be peace in the plant world and in the forests. Let the cosmic powers be peaceful. Let the Brahman, the true essence and source of life, be peaceful. Let there be undiluted and fulfilling peace everywhere.'
— A prayer from the *Atharva Veda*,
one of Hinduism's most sacred texts

Worship of natural elements such as fire (agni), Earth (dharti) as the mother, and water (pani) is very common in many rituals. In prayers, Hindus ask for peace on Earth and peace for all the living organisms including plants and animals.

Here are two examples of Hindu mantras which link people to Mother Earth:

1. Om, that (Divine power) which pervades the Bhu Loka (Earth as the Physical Plane),
   Bhuvar Loka (outside Earth/sky Antariksha Loka) and Suvar Loka (Swarga Loka or heaven or the Celestial Plane),
   That Savitr (Divine Illumination) which is the Most Adorable,
   On that Divine Radiance we meditate,

May that enlighten our intellect and awaken our spiritual wisdom.

2. Om, may there be peace in heaven,
   May there be peace in the sky,
   May there be peace on Earth,
   May there be peace in the water,
   May there be peace in the plants,
   May there be peace in the trees,
   May there be peace in the gods in the various worlds,
   May there be peace in Brahman,
   May there be peace in all,
   May there be peace indeed within peace,
   Giving me the peace which grows within me, Om, peace, peace, peace.

In Hinduism, many mantras and preachings link us directly with Mother Earth, water, air and fire; these elements are worshipped at many occasions. There are four Vedas which are large bodies of text in ancient India, and these connect human existence with nature and ultimately with God. Apart from the four Vedas, Upanishads also present a huge knowledge base for mankind that helps us connect with natural elements.

Islam

According to the Islamic faith, Allah (God) has created all the various creatures on Earth and we should see God in all the creatures so that we look after them.

- 'He created the skies and the Earth for truth. He coils the night upon the day, and He coils the day upon the night.' — *Qur'an 39:5*
- 'The world is green and beautiful, and Allah has appointed you his guardian over it,' taught the prophet Muhammad.

- 'No creature is there crawling on the Earth, no bird flying with its wings, but they are nations like unto yourselves. We have neglected nothing in the Book; then to their Lord they shall be mustered.' — *Qur'an 6:38*
- '...He created everything and determined them in exact proportions.' — *Qur'an 25:2*

Sikhism

Sikhism believes that nature is God's creation. All the different components of nature perform according to the Almighty, and all these components are well aligned and organised. The different parts of the universe are in His order, including our galaxy, planet and other parts. One famous aarti (prayer) is:

'Gopal tero aarta.....', where Gopal is the Almighty and all the vegetation on this earth performs aarti of the Almighty.

'*Pavan guru, pani pita, mata dharat mahat,*' is a prayer recited in the mornings that translates as 'air is our guru, water is our father and Earth is our mother'. This prayer reminds us that people are just a small part of a whole universal system.

'I am a sacrifice to your almighty creative power which is pervading everywhere.' — The First Guru, Guru Nanak, confirming the presence of the Creator in His creation (nature). The main principles of Sikhism, as Guru Nanak Dev ji stated, are enforcing the idea of being in harmony with nature:

1. Kirat Karo: work hard, live honestly, truthfully and follow the truth.
2. Vand Sako: share with others and have contentment in life.
3. Naam Japo: remember the Almighty, follow the truth and always analyse what is right/wrong in the light of a clear conscience (truth).

These principles are based on being content in life and leading a spiritual life in harmony with nature.

The Sikh gurus have taught about caring for nature and made their followers aware of their responsibility towards the environment. It includes examples: to promote agriculture one should produce their own food, do good deeds, share the produce and help the needy people as a part of dharma and karma. Karma involves being good with nature and its various components. A common kitchen to share food with all, irrespective of any caste/background etc., is a very good example of sustainable environmental living that one can see in any Sikh temple. There is no difference between the world of humans and the world of nature, and both of these are equally important and must be treated with respect.

Zoroastrism

Zoroastrism is an ancient Iranian religion and religious philosophy. Zoroastrians claim to be the world's first proponent of ecology, and they care for the elements of nature and the Earth. The Zoroastrian faith promotes the caring of the physical world not just to seek spiritual salvation but also for humans to be seen as the natural motivators or overseers of God's 'Seven Creations', that is, the sky, water, Earth, plants, animals, humans and fire. Zoroastrianism sees the physical world as a natural matrix of the Seven Creations in which life and growth are inter-dependent if harmony and perfection are to be the final goal.

I acknowledge there are many other religions in the world that may also preach similar kinds of lessons for humankind. Apart from these religions mentioned above, there are also many tribal societies with similar teachings on how to live with, and respect, Mother Nature. My concern is despite our fine religious preachings; we don't follow the right path to satisfy our needs to live. Our nature of over-exploitation or maximising our benefits takes over all the other things, and we end up exploiting Mother Nature. We certainly lack application of our religious and scientific knowledge on environmental issues. One main aspect that could help us to connect and apply this knowledge is spirituality.

Spirituality and nature

Spirituality is such an important aspect of human life because it allows us to explore and improve ourselves. Spirituality cannot exist without nature. Nature is a fundamental part of our spiritual experiences whether one believes in religion or not. This service by nature is irreplaceable, and it is beyond any price. There is so much to learn from the natural processes, living organisms and from the interactions between the various organisms.

As an example, a tropical rainforest can teach us how to live with each other and to share the resources. I am always fascinated to consider the dual functions of any little patch in a rainforest, where on one hand it serves humans by providing good air, shade and shelter, beauty etc., and on the other hand it harbours many different types of species. Consider a small area (say about 2 m2) of the rainforest in the tropics. There may be 10–20 plant species growing in the small area, with hundreds of other fauna visiting and/or living on this patch. The plant species that grow in such an environment occupy every little bit of land that is available. They try to reach out for the sunlight by taking the support of a big tree. One such big tree may support 50–100 other species that grow on its branches, leaves, bark and underneath.

Although, tropical soils are poor in nutrients, many plant and other species live in co-operation with each other, and they are able to support each other and many other wild fauna for providing food and habitat. Although there will be some competition among these species for available resources, usually such species adapt themselves in a way that they all survive (for example, some grow straight to the top, others twine, some adapt to survive in less sunlight while others may restrict to the base for greater moisture content). Adaptation is a significant force in nature that many living organisms have followed through evolution while humans have lost the capability to adapt to nature, and instead we attempt to change nature to meet our needs.

I believe that humans could adopt the same attitude as the various floral and faunal species do in the tropical forest, by supporting and co-operating with each other. We certainly need to change our current attitude for material collection and exploiting resources for maximum individual gain or to make the environment suit our needs. We do not need all the materials that we gather for which we spend precious time out of our life. We need to learn to enhance our human capabilities by being co-operative and supportive, to sustain ourselves on this planet which provides us with the basic life support system. I quite agree with Sen (1981) who said there would be no famine on Earth if we knew how to manage our food and related resources.

If we change our attitudes and values towards the use of

resources and if we learn to adapt ourselves to nature rather than making changes to nature to suit our needs, we will all realise how easy it is for us and our future generations to survive on the planet Earth. An ethical approach to preserving our natural resources, as earlier adopted by our ancestors and indigenous societies, could be a way forward for all of us to preserve our precious resources.

The Dalai Lama said, 'You see, taking care of the planet is nothing special, nothing sacred and nothing holy. It is something like taking care of our own house. We have no other planet or house except this one. Although there are a lot of disturbances and problems, this is our only alternative.' Ultimately, it's about controlling our desires and only collecting materials that we really need. Once we learn to satisfy ourselves with the materials and define our limits, there will be less pressure on our natural systems and we can certainly sustain our resources.

As Gandhi ii also said, 'There is enough for everyone's need, but not for their greed.'

Lessons to be learnt from Indigenous Australians

'The land owns you, and you have to look after it ...'
— Mayr Darkie

'Trees and animals, they're like our brothers and sisters;
we got to care for them; they are part of us too.'
— Colin Lawrence, Kowanyama

There is a lot that we can learn from Indigenous people. As stated in Chapter 1, the Indigenous way of living is intricately linked with nature for various cultural, spiritual and other activities. Land, considered as 'mother', is cared for with a sense of responsibility. During hunting/food gathering activities, the elders taught the younger generation bush skills, passed on knowledge about plants, animals and the country, and told stories about the land and their elders.

Land is not a separate entity for Indigenous people but rather there is a 'oneness' between people and land. The land forms the identity of the people, of their elders and of their future generations. As Father Dave Passi, a plaintiff in the Mabo land rights' judgment, said, 'It is my father's land, my grandfather's land, my grandmother's land. I am related to it; it gives me my identity. If I don't fight for it, then I will be moved out of it and [it] will be the loss of my identity.'

For Indigenous people, their lands and waters underpin who they are and the foundation of their very survival as people. Indigenous people all over the globe also insist that living things cannot be separated from the land they grow on, and that people's knowledge and myriad uses of natural resources cannot be separated from their culture (Jean 1995).

The presence of various plants and animals is also important in various relationships among people, in the Dreamtime stories, and in connections with the country. Many ceremonial activities are linked to land or water. Being on land provides the opportunity for people to be together to perform rituals, cultural ceremonies and to keep their spiritual relationships with the country (Muir 1998). Sacredness of land is mentioned often in the Dreamtime stories for various events, as Indigenous man Kenny Jimmy says, 'the stories go along with the land, everything, must go ... so ... you are talking about land and all that ... our stories gotta be there to cover all our land' (Strang 2000).

Traditions, history and relations linked with sacred sites are passed on from one generation to another and are of paramount importance for the wellbeing of a society. About the Indigenous people living in the north-eastern Arnhem Land (the Yolngu people), Mick Dodson (1997, cited in Williams 1998, pg. 4) said, 'our traditional relationship to land is profoundly spiritual.'

Dhayirra Yunupingu (Williams 1998, pg. 5) from the same community explains about sacredness of the land '... this land of ours, it provided our ceremonial objects, sacred for people, and it wasn't the only sacred things which were given but the land also provided the sacred names, the kinship, the subsections, the homelands, and whatever language you might speak. So wherever we Yolngu people see this land, we must care for it as if it were our mother.' According to Indigenous culture, land provides a medium through which all aspects of life are mediated, and they manage land for both spiritual and physical values to keep the country healthy for future generations.

Over the past thousands of years of use, Australia's Indigenous people have developed knowledge of different plants and animals. Many authors have written about the bush food and medicine. Keen (2004) described the environments and resources for the Indigenous people from seven different communities. Among these, two are in the savanna country, that is, Ngarinyin (in north-east of Australia) and Yolngu people (north-Arnhem lands). Both of these communities use various plant species for vegetable food, seeds, nuts and for fruits, and have knowledge of when and how to harvest plant products according to the climate. Isaacs (1987) describes their knowledge about flora and fauna as:

Aboriginal people have an encyclopedic knowledge of Australian plants and animals and of seasonal changes in the Australian environment. A batwing coral tree flowers, its orange blossoms fall and women know it is time to go and dig crabs from their hides under the mangrove mud. Their fat, too, will be orange, and the flesh good and filling. Another flower blooms to warn that poisonous stringers are in the northern waters, while the milky white flowers known as 'oyster flowers' tell people to move camp to the oyster beds, for the oysters are fat and white. Every child learns the importance of such natural signs. The winds, the blooming of plants and the seeding of grasses, rather than a fixed calendar of dates and months, herald the changes of seasons. (Isaacs 1987, pg. 13).

From an ecological perspective, the feeling of 'oneness' and 'relatedness' to land among Aboriginal people helps them follow practices that sustain the land resources. This seems to be the main reason that Indigenous communities do not exploit the resources, and instead they integrated themselves with nature to co-exist as one entity (Fig. 5.4).

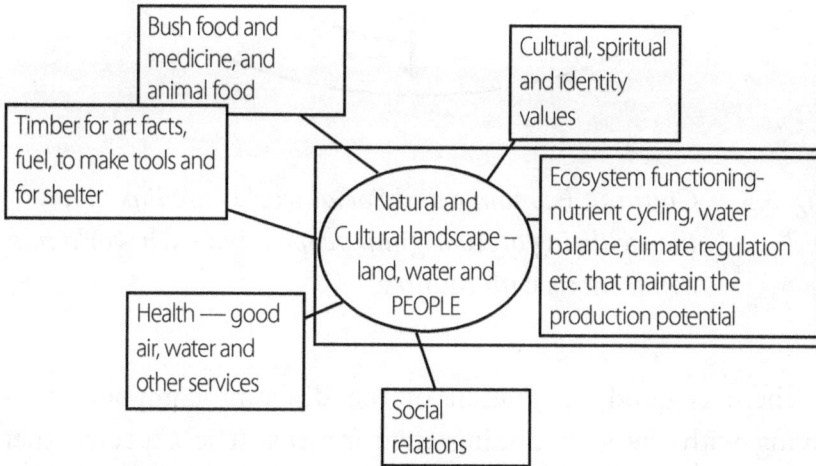

Fig. 5.4: *Indigenous links with the natural systems and people's wellbeing (a conceptual framework).*

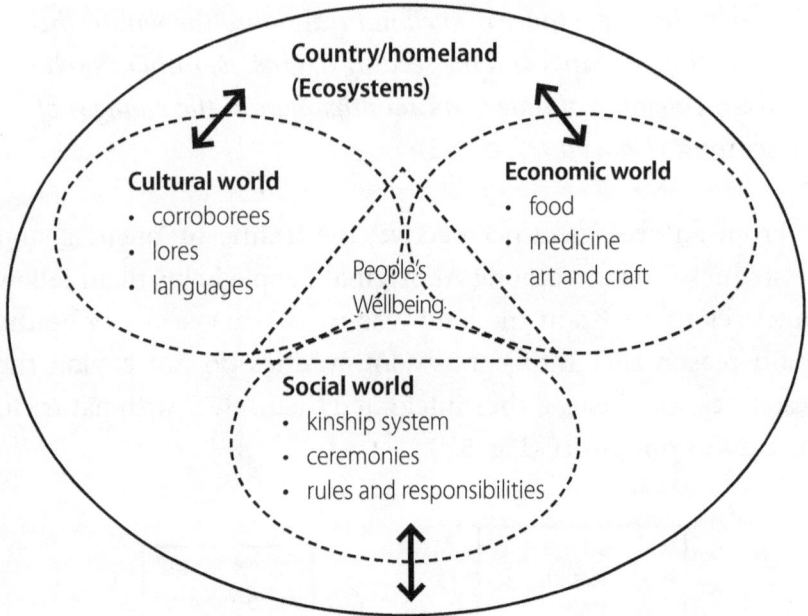

Fig. 5.5: *Cultural, Economic and Social worlds are linked to the wellbeing of Aboriginal people, and each world has connections with country.*

There is good integration of the different components of living with the surrounding environment. It is expected that people from different countries/homelands will have variations in their knowledge, use and management of resources. Overall, Indigenous people's wellbeing is well integrated with the natural resources as shown in Fig. 5.5.

What lessons we can learn from Australia's Indigenous people:

1. Use of native plants could be a way forward for many of us to learn how we can live in harmony with nature. For example, many bushes and trees have been commonly used by Indigenous people as shown in Table 5.1:

Table 5.1: Food value of some common Australian native plants.

Botanical name	Common name	Use
Acacia spp.	Wattle	Seeds are exceptionally nutritious, with higher protein and fat contents even than wheat or rice. Gum is a good source of dietary fibre.
Acmena smithii	Lillypilly	Fruits (berries) are widely eaten, as these are a good source of water and minerals.
Adansonia gregorii	Baobab nut	Seeds and pith are eaten raw and with honey.
Alpinia spp.	Wild ginger	Buds, stems and roots eaten raw, and leaves are used for flavouring.
Ampelocissus acetosa	Native grape	Fruit is eaten raw, and thick roots are eaten after cooking.
Banksia dentata	Swamp banksia	Nectar from flowers is sucked, or flowers are also soaked in water to prepare sweet liquid.
Boerhavia diffusa	Tar vine	Root are roasted in fire and considered a good source of food (for its water and carbohydrate content).
Brachychiton spp.	Kurrajong	Water-bearing trees, roots are tapped for water in drought. Seeds are mostly eaten.
Buchanania obovata	Wild plum	Fruits are a good source of vitamin C and are eaten raw.
Cycas media	Cycad	Nuts are dried, soaked, fermented and then roasted.
Dioscorea spp.	Yam	Underground tubers are a good source of water, carbohydrates, protein and some trace elements.

Botanical name	Common name	Use
Eucalyptus spp.	Gumtree and others	Many eucalypt species are used to extract water from roots/bark, for nectar and seeds.
Ficus spp.	Fig	Fruits from all the species are eaten raw.
Livistona australis	Cabbage tree palm	Young shoots and leaves are eaten raw.
Nymphaea sp.	Waterlily	Seeds, bulbs and stems are eaten.
Many other species are also used by the Aboriginal people as listed in many reference books (Aboriginal communities of the Northern Territory of Australia 1988, Isaacs 1987, Cribb and Cribb 1975, 1981 and 1982, Low 1989 and Levitt 1981).		

Similarly many common species have medicinal values, some of which are listed in the table below (Table 5.2):

Table 5.2. Medicinal uses of some common Australian native plants.

Botanical name	Common name	Medicinal use
Acacia spp. (*many species*)	Wattle	Bark used for decoction of skin conditions such as boils. Gum mixed with bark is used to treat wounds and sores.
Acacia ligulata	Wattle	Bark is boiled or soaked and drunk as cough medicine. Also good for sickness ('smoking' ill people), dizziness, nerves and fits.
Alphitonia excelsa	Red ash	Young leaf tips chewed for upset stomach and decoction of bark and wood used as liniment for muscular pains or gargles to relieve toothache.

Botanical name	Common name	Medicinal use
Alstonia constricta	Quinine bush	A deadly poison. Latex used to cure infectious sores though very severe on the skin.
Brachychiton diversifolium	Kurrajong	Inner bark crushed in water and the liquid is used as an eye wash.
Buchanania obovata	Wild plum	Leaves crushed and applied to sores, boils, wounds and ringworms. Inner bark and sapwood pounded and soaked and used for toothaches. Ashes of burnt sapwood are packed around the sore tooth.
Capparis lasiantha	Native orange/Bush caper	Honey from flowers is used as a remedy for coughs. Plant, including roots, macerated and soaked, and water applied to swellings, snake bites, insect bites and stings.
Cycas media	Cycad	Used especially for spear wounds. Soft nsides of the male flower stalk are combined with human urine in a paperbark container to heat liquid which is then used as an antiseptic.
Erythrophleum chlorostachyum	Ironwood, Cooktown poison tree	Leaves boiled in water to bathe sores and cuts. Infusions from bark and roots are used to treat sores and stomach ache. Wood, leaves and bark were used to 'smoke' person suffering from constipation. Pulverised leaves placed in nostrils to relieve diarrhoea.
Eucalyptus spp.	Gumtree and others	Gum is extracted from many trees to treat sores, cuts, as an astringent, and for cold and cough.

Botanical name	Common name	Medicinal use
Ficus opposita	Sandpaper fi	Eyewash made by soaking inner bark in water. Leaves are used to treat inflammation. Infusion is drunk to treat diarrhoea.
Hibiscus tiliaceous	Yellow hibiscus, cottonwood	Decoction of the inner bark and sapwood is used to wash wounds. Bark is used to wrap around wounds.
Pandanus spiralis	Screw palm	Inner core of a young tree is eaten to cure diarrhoea. Upper inner core of trees is used to treat colds, toothaches and wounds.
Spinifex longifolius	Spinifex	Juice squeezed from new shoots is used to cure sore eyes. Decoction of young shoots is used to treat infected sores or burns.
Terminalia ferdinandiana	Billygoat/ Green/ Kakadu plum	Inner bark is used to cure sores, leprosy sores, and backache.

Many other species used by the Aboriginal people to treat many ailments are mentioned in reference books (Cribb and Cribb 1981 and 1982, Isaacs 1987 and Lassak and McCarthy 1983).

2. To adapt ourselves to live with nature by adjusting our habits, needs and learning ways so that we don't exploit our natural resources.
3. To connect ourselves with the land in ways that promote our spiritual and emotional connections with the country.

The natural resources play a significant role in shaping the fabric of Indigenous societies and their wellbeing. However, in the present times, Indigenous living is well exposed to the external pressures and modern lifestyle choices, and has changed notably. For the last 100–150 years, even though many Indigenous people have modified their lifestyle, interestingly many still retain their connections to land for various ceremonial, cultural and sacred activities that play a significant role in their wellbeing.

Unfortunately, most of these connections are missing when we measure the wellbeing of Indigenous people. A socio-economic-ecological measure that includes how people value natural resources would actually be an effective tool to reflect the wellbeing of many Indigenous people. This could also suit many non-Indigenous people that value these resources in their wellbeing. We are very fortunate to have Indigenous people living in Australia who have the knowledge and skills to manage our fragile natural resources and have survived the harsh conditions over the last 50,000–60,000 years. There is a need to integrate traditional and scientific information, ultimately to benefit all of us, to understand and value our connections with nature.

Importance of Land: a song by Neprrjna Gumbula (1994) on 'Yolngu Children':

...Can't you hear the Yolngu children
Crying out for freedom and rights
This land and its heritage
Has been handed back again
Yolngu children must live in the Yolngu way of life
We have fought back the land for our new generation
Its beauty and the land of ours will remain the same
For the future of Yolngu children

(Corn and Gumbula 2001, pg. 57)

In conclusion, this chapter highlights how our wellbeing is related with nature. Our spiritual connections with nature are particularly important as these are irreplaceable and beyond any price tag. The major religions in the world also teach us to live in harmony with nature. This view matches very well with the ecological principles that promote an eco-centric way of living. An eco-centric way of living is nature-centered in contrast to our current human-centered way of living. To do so, there are important lessons to be learnt from our Indigenous people.

Overall, integration of our economic and social world will assist us to better understand the role of nature in our living.

6

The future:
A hybrid model for sustainable, holistic living

'Every day, think as you wake up, today I am fortunate to be alive, I have a precious human life; I am not going to waste it.'

— The Dalai Lama

This chapter is all about applying solutions for sustainable living, thus aiming to make our lives more meaningful. We have precious natural resources to support our livelihoods. We have discussed a range of socio-economic interactions between nature and human living in the previous chapters. Now the important question is about how to apply our knowledge. Our strength is that we are aware of our environmental issues, and to some extent we realise that our living is dependent upon natural systems. Our limitation is that despite our awareness, we are an 'intensive resource-use' society on Earth, and we like to change nature rather than adapting ourselves to suit nature's ways. Without doubt, we lack the application of our knowledge in the modern era. To learn how to apply our knowledge, I suggest a few easy ways, and I am sure that you can easily come up with many more ways. It just requires inspiration!

I propose a hybrid model to enhance our living through various sustainable and holistic ways that suit the modern world. With recent advances in technology, we can efficiently use our resources, unlike in the earlier industrial times when a large number of resources were wasted. In the past, the availability of resources and our attitude to valuing natural resources, led to overuse. However, now we are realising the value of our natural resources in our day-to-day living and know that we are facing the consequences, whether it is in the form of changes in weather patterns, severe climatic events or changes in our agricultural production systems.

Advances in technology could play a significant role in reducing our impact on natural resources. We can take advantage of new technologies to generate less waste and make more efficient use of resources. For example, treatment and/or recycling of wastewater, recycling of paper and plastic materials, efficiency in fuel consumption, generation of renewable energy etc. have been greatly helpful at a household as well as at a local or regional scale. A change in our attitude and application of new knowledge coupled with new technologies can help us to be wise citizens of our Earth. I believe that we can achieve this by implementing changes in our own day-to-day living and applying a holistic perspective to life. If every one of us puts in the effort to change, we can enhance our wellbeing and protect Mother Earth for the present and future generations!

The main aspects of living a life in harmony with nature are that we consider ourselves a part of nature (not a superpower that can rule/control nature), cooperate with each other for use of resources, value our resources, limit our aspirations, adapt to nature and connect ourselves to our natural surroundings. We follow an eco-centric path of living while fulfilling our modern day-to-day duties. A hybrid model for such a life includes the following main components for our wellbeing:

1. ecology,
2. economics,
3. social, and
4. healthy and spiritual living.

These four components are very interconnected, but generally we hardly realise those connections. Ecology (the study of our household) and Economics (the management of our household) are both related. A 'household' is not just the constructed house (a building) in which we live, but also the 'actual' domiciliary that provides us with food, air, water, and a good emotional and physical environment, etc. This household that I am referring to includes the support system on Earth that provides us with the basic needs for living. It could be our own backyard, a farm, or other agriculture or nature-related places. Often, we limit our thinking to the 'house' we live in but forget that we need much more than just a house to live. So when we think about protecting the household that helps us survive, it is important to broaden our perspectives to consider nature and its systems as part of our household.

We need to be aware of how our basic needs are fulfilled. We discussed this in detail in the ecology section (Chapter 2). Ecology plays a significant role in our healthy and spiritual living as it does in our household economics and social lives. If we have good air to breathe, good food to eat, good water to drink and good environmental surroundings, we can lead healthy lives, which will have positive impacts on our social and economic wellbeing.

As the Dalai Lama said, 'we first spend our health and energy to gather money, and then we earn money to recuperate our health. We are so worried about living in comfort for the future that we do not live in the present, and by the old age we have wasted all our time and energy. We live as if we are never going to die, and then we die without really living. We do not realise the reality of our lives — that death is always approaching near to us!' This is so true when we think about what we do in our day-to-day lives. Most of us are running the rat race without considering the future implications.

In the modern world, the economy is the main driver. We are

trapped and fascinated by the modern comforts of life and strive constantly to get one comfort after another. For example, if I buy a 'good' car for comfort, then I also look for a house where I have a garage to park that good car, and then I look for nice seat covers or other items for the car. Similarly, if I buy a nice house then there are certainly many more things to look for, and this list can go on and on. Though we work hard to achieve what we want and to be economically well off, we also waste a lot of our time and energy, as this approach does not enhance our wellbeing. As I mentioned before, we miss learning about ourselves and living a balanced life.

Given that the modern world is very much dominated by 'materialistic thinking', a 'consumerism-oriented economy' and a 'showoff' attitude and values, it is hard for anyone to lead life diffe ently, particularly for the younger generation. The modern economy, with its focus on consumerism rather than on the actual wellbeing of individuals, plays a significant role in directing our lives. I believe it is very important today for our younger generation to learn those basic techniques for living a balanced and contented life within our given resources. It requires a change in our education system including the introduction of new courses that focus on learning balanced life strategies in schools and universities.

If we get our economics right, that means if we holistically think about our 'wellbeing', consolidate our aspirations, apply spirituality and learn how to live happily within our resources, we will not over-consume our resources. We can make ourselves safe from the 'trap' of materialistic items by keeping in mind the ultimate ends and means of life (see ultimate means and ends figure discussed earlier). By controlling our aspirations, we can enjoy the present and can lead healthy and creative lives.

Living in harmony with nature can be the key to achieving a healthy and creative life. It can be achieved in many ways, e.g. by growing herbs, fruits and vegetables in our backyards, particularly if we are living in suburban areas, and by visiting natural areas, etc. We can also lead a creative life by working with the soil which puts us closer to Mother Nature. It is a kind of meditation. It also gives us a peace of mind and sets things in the context of time and space. Time is a major factor when we sow, grow or harvest plants. This simple exercise will help us to understand the importance of 'time' and 'change'.

Time also brings change and various components of nature to adapt to the changes in the seasons. Learning this will help us to develop an ability to adapt to changes that are part of natural processes. Moreover, we will become more aware of climate change as we concern ourselves with the plants we grow in our backyards. There are some small economic benefits to growing a garden, but there are many more indirect economic benefits, including accessing good quality food, peace of mind and living a healthy and spiritual life.

I take the example of gardening that I do to produce some herbs, vegetables and fruit in our backyard. You could similarly do yours. I calculated a replacement cost for these goods I obtained from my backyard (which otherwise I would have bought from the supermarket) of roughly $10 per week for raspberries, spinach, bok choy, silverbeet, tomatoes, chilies, corn, mint, coriander, chives and a few others. There are some special plants I grow that I can't get from the market, so their value is much more than just the market price. Moreover, these items are produced using our household green waste, without any external inputs (chemical fertilisers). This exercise of gardening makes me aware of the changing seasons. Moreover, the produce is fresh, chemical-free and reliable, and the process also keeps me busy, providing some benefits for spiritual and healthy living — these services are beyond any price tag. This also provides an opportunity for my children to learn gardening and to share their produce with others. In the summer of 2015, my younger daughter picked a small basket of raspberries every morning and took them to her classmates for sharing. All the children in her class looked forward to her raspberries since the season started that year. She is learning a good habit of collecting raspberries and then sharing her produce with others. This home gardening exercise also gives me the opportunity to share our garden produce with neighbours and friends, thus helping in socialisation.

This little activity at the household level provides me with economic, social and health benefits. My total monetary benefits are approximately $40 per month or $500 per year while my health, social and spiritual benefits are beyond price. If I evaluate the actual cost, the savings for me working in our garden are huge. Otherwise, I would have spent that time in a supermarket buying fruits and vegetables and then drinking a cup of coffee or tea in a shop that indirectly costs me possibly $1000 per year. In a way, I save that time and spend it to lead my creative life (as I aspire to do).

However, one can easily say that buying those items from the supermarket is much easier, and we can spend time on having a relaxed cup of coffee with family or friends. Again, the question is about our personal attitude, our values and the choices we make. We need to develop an attitude that embraces our values, usages and activities in relation to nature. There is a need for a fresh look at life from a new perspective to lead creative lives. Another invaluable lesson acquired from gardening is that my children are also learning to play with nature by growing their seeds and caring for them — a skill they may not be able to learn in school.

I believe doing things together and involving family and children in our activities can help us all in terms of health, social life and learning about nature. We may have enough money to spend on a cup of coffee or to buy items from a supermarket rather than growing them ourselves, but the question is about holistic learning and creating a change in our attitude and values.

We need to value the connections with nature that provide not just produce but many other benefits (given we have the skills, opportunity and a desire to grow plants at home). Ultimately it is our attitude and mindset. If we train our minds to measure benefits beyond the monetary terms, we can certainly achieve desired results. I believe we can all get time to inculcate this new attitude, and we need the 'will' to do so! If we assess the value of home produce in terms of money only without evaluating the associated non-monetary benefits (health, spiritual, social and others), then we fail to change our attitude. If we incorporate the value of these associated benefits, then the real value of producing our own fruits and vegetables is much greater than just comparing it with the market price.

Growing our own fruits and vegetables, even on a small scale, working with soil and experiencing the changes in the seasons, will give us real socio-economic and health benefits. It is also a good way to enhance our social lives. I have made friends with neighbours down the street that cultivate home gardens also. We exchange several items such as mandarins, spinach, coriander, mint, garlic and ginger. On a community level, growing useful plants can initiate community groups. For example, for farming and grazing communities in Australia, there are already Landcare groups in almost every town. Similarly, there could be 'backyard cultivation' groups in each town which many urban cities lack.

We could also start community gardening on parklands. There are some community gardening groups in big cities such as Brisbane, Sydney and Canberra, but the concept is not very common among the general population and is nearly non-existent in small towns. Community gardening could be a wonderful experience, especially for those who do not have the skills to do it at home or who feel shy to start with. For young families, it may be difficult to make the time and energy to visit the community gardens, but it could equally be a fun time for children to learn and play in their own backyards. Another option is to start backyard cultivation groups in the suburbs.

There are many benefits to backyard cultivation, as it does not require the time and energy to visit a community garden. When we grow vegetables or herbs at home, we can just pick them up when we cook. Moreover, one can work in the garden whenever one has the time, and it provides excellent learning and fun opportunities for young children.

However, for inexperienced people, community gardens are a good way to start. The purpose of these groups is to enhance the practise of gardening through communication and socialisation among people. Moreover, people will get the opportunity to start growing their own vegetables, herbs and fruits, and to communicate with each other to enhance their knowledge and skills about what to cultivate, how to cultivate or when to cultivate.

Backyard and community gardening efforts would initiate a common platform for many people living in the urban and suburban areas. There is a need for government initiatives to help these groups thrive, at the household as well as at the community level.

Community gardens

Developing gardens on common land is a great concept. Gardens can be set up in parks, botanical gardens or any other place that is accessible to the public. There have been a few initiatives by the Australian government to set up community gardens. However, the concept is still not common among the general public.

A group of like-minded people can start such a garden. An important aspect of community gardens is to ensure the produce is edible and usable by people. For example, fruit trees, herbs, vegetables and some floriculture plants will keep people interested in the garden, as they can obtain produce for all their hard work. Involving young children in the garden activities will provide an opportunity to develop an interest in gardening, knowledge and a feeling of belongingness.

Involving children will also help us to teach our future generations not only how to cultivate produce, but also to realise the importance of our connections with nature and its processes, and to learn about the impacts of climate change on the future.

I used to have a little section of herb garden in my house when I was a young child that was always special to me. I felt responsible for looking after that part of the garden. It provided me with a sense of belongingness, responsibility, caring and working to produce something (mostly herbs and vegetables) that our family could use. Along with this, I also developed a sense of awareness about the climate in my childhood; I still remember I used to worry about water availability, the dry season and high temperatures and how that would affect my plants. It made me feel proud whenever some herbs from my garden were used in cooking food for the family.

There are multiple benefits to gardening for the younger generation, especially for our children. It provides a great opportunity for them to learn gardening skills including cultivation of plants and herbs in their own yards and knowledge of how to make use of those plants, which will give them at least some level of satisfaction and happiness. Moreover, this practise of watching their parents and guardians growing plants will help children learn lifelong skills that they can apply to their lives. Working with soil is a meditating activity that can assist many children to calm down and to be with themselves. Gardening can also be turned into a play activity by assigning children an area and allowing them to learn to sow, care and to look after their plants. This kind of exercise will also help them to learn about the relaxation that can be obtained from working with the soil and being a part of nature.

Our ecology, economics, health and spiritual living are all interconnected. Working to produce your own food helps household economics, provides healthy food and exercise for a healthy lifestyle, as well as providing spiritual opportunities. We need to realise those connections, not just for the monetary financial benefits but also for many intangible benefits that cannot be priced. This can help us keep the life spectrum of ultimate means and ultimate ends in place since we will be in touch with nature to produce some of our required materials and our minds will be relaxed and at peace.

People's power to create change for healthy and sustainable living

Each and every individual's effort will matter if we start implementing change for a better future for ourselves and for our children.

Imagine a suburb where everyone is growing some kind of fruit, vegetable or herb in their gardens. People will start sharing knowledge and skills. They will share and exchange their produce, even though this may be in small quantities. The process of cultivating plants in one's own backyard will enhance socialisation among people. It could be particularly useful for older people who do not have many opportunities to meet and talk with young people. This will provide a new experience for everyone, both for old and young, and will create a sense of belongingness for children growing up in a suburb where people know each other, trust each other and share their home garden produce. It is rare to see such situations in urban areas, but in some rural areas it is still visible.

In this kind of co-operative setting, children can play a significant role in bringing people together. In return, their upbringing will be very different in many positive ways than those who are confined to spending time indoors on computers or iPads. Knowing the community where they live and grow, will provide children with a different sense of belongingness, security and responsibility. It will provide them with the lifelong benefit of knowing people from different age groups rather than just their own parents (as happens in many situations). This will certainly help children to acquire social and networking skills just by observing and doing things with the people that surround them. So, many problems of our children that include mental, social, or health could be minimised to a certain degree.

The most important aspect of such an activity will be 'instilling a sense of community' among people living in an area where people know each other and can trust each other. This will improve many social skills and contribute to our development from both a social and personal perspective. Imagine a child growing in this kind of free and trustworthy environment. He or she is certainly going to have little problem interacting with other people and will have the confidence and ability to understand different perspectives on life rather than the one aspect that he or she experiences at home with their parents. If there are good people in a neighbourhood, all this is possible to do, and people will achieve all the possible health and social benefits, but we need to have the will to enact change. We have many examples throughout the world where people enacted change and achieved their outcomes, whether that was saving trees from being cut, saving animals or saving people.

This community gardening initiative can change the lives of both children and adults in many positive ways, and our future society could be quite different than what it is today. Some of our social problems such as lack of interaction, building trust, spending time indoors playing computer games, etc. will no longer be such an issue if this plan is enacted. I am not a social scientist, but I am sure that if we incorporate natural components in our current ways of living, then our socio-economic life and health will be much better than what we currently experience. There will be many flow-on benefits for individuals, groups and for all of us as a society. We will be on the right path for 'development', in its deep sense of leading creative and healthy lives!

Actions needed for 'change':

1. To instill working habits to grow vegetables, fruits and herbs in the backyard.
2. To involve family members, particularly children, in activities for planting.
3. To communicate knowledge with neighbours and friends about cultivating plants.
4. To share the produce that comes from the backyard with friends, family members and neighbours.
5. To share the experience with others.
6. To set up 'backyard cultivation' groups in each suburban and urban area.

Flow-on benefits from such an initiative include:

1. Health benefits from working in the yard, producing and consuming good quality produce and learning new skills.
2. Spiritual benefits from working with soil and being in connection with nature.
3. Economic benefits from spending less money in the

supermarkets and producing your own vegetables, herbs and fruits.

4. Opportunity to socialise with others, to share knowledge and skills, and to learn from others' experiences.
5. Instilling the healthy habit of eating fresh vegetables and herbs, especially for those who mainly rely on meat products.
6. Savings on medical expenses due to good dietary habits.
7. Learning new skills for plant cultivation.
8. Socialising with neighbours and friends.
9. An awareness of climate change and its impact on the plants we grow and on food crops that farmers grow for all of us.
10. Reducing the amount of waste we produce by growing our own fruits and vegetables.
11. Creating a safe environment for the present and future generations.
12. Realising our connections with nature.
13. Enhancing our wellbeing to lead creative and healthy lives.

The above example is from a gardening perspective, but you can choose similar other actions just as for 'zero fuel consumption' or 'zero plastic waste', etc. that you may like to do and estimate its total possible benefits.

People, as a group, have a lot of power and can make a significant difference. We need to change our attitude and habits now before it's too late. Ultimately, it is our responsibility to save our Earth for future generations, as it is the only home we can live in. There is a saying 'if we win our own mind and control our aspirations; we can bring the change'. So, let's control our minds and aspirations, and live a fruitful life. Our willingness to create 'change' at an individual level could help all of us to solve many environmental problems and advance a sustainable way of living for all of us!

In conclusion, I wish I could contribute to bringing a little change in your mind to start thinking about 'doing something' that is in harmony with nature. Any little action on your behalf could become a big change for the society you live in, for your children and elders in the family and for the broader community. We just need to start realising the importance of nature in our lives and the immense benefits that we can enjoy. We all need to move away from the current dis-connected approach of wellbeing towards a more holistic approach to wellbeing that promotes our sustainable living on planet Earth. Many aspects of our life will sort out automatically once we are at peace with ourselves and with Mother Nature!

The time to act is now! We are a knowledgeable society, and we need to apply our knowledge now. Let's all do our best to live in harmony with nature for ourselves and for our future generations. Let's all promise that I, as an individual, will do my best to reduce the resource use and to reduce the waste production. A change will certainly occur! Let's be an integral part of this change and lead our creative and healthy lives.

Appendix 1:

Example: I have highlighted the use of various natural resources in my day-to-day living by providing examples in Chapter 2, and you can also do the same by answering the questions in the questionnaire below:

Q 1. What do you need to start your day? List the main items and where they come from.

Q2. What is the most important drink that you need and its components?

Q3. What do you eat for breakfast and where does each and every item come from?

Q4. What do you usually have for lunch, snacks and dinner? Consider the ingredients, their origin and list all in a table.

Q5. What are the vital things in life that help you to live contently and/or a healthy life?

Q6. What are the other things you need for healthy living and hygiene?

Q7. What activities do you like to do e.g. walking, riding, visiting a park etc.?

Q8. What is most important in your life: money, nature, or a mix of the two, and how?

Q9. What is the most critical thing in our living without which we can't live — nature or money (define your priorities and think thoroughly)?

Q10. What do you do in your everyday life that helps to repay Mother Nature?

Assessment of the daily use of natural resources:

Item	Requirement in terms of necessity:		
	Low (can survive without it)	Medium	High (can't live without it)
Water: purpose Drink Cleansing Toileting			
Air: purpose Breathe Breeze Wind (for crop pollination)			
Clothes			
Food: Herbs/vegetables Meat/eggs/cheese Grains/cereals Milk			
Shelter: 1. House			

References

Aboriginal communities of the Northern Territory of Australia. (1988). *Traditional bush medicines — An Aboriginal pharmacopoeia*. Greenhouse publications, Victoria.

Australian Bureau of Statistics (ABS). (2001). *Measuring wellbeing: frameworks for Australian Social Statistics*. ABS catalogue no. 4160.0. Australian Bureau of Statistics, Canberra.

ABS. (2009). *Environmental issues: People's views and practices*. Catalogue no. 4602. Australian Bureau of Statistics, Canberra.

ABS. (2010). *Australia's environment: issues and trends*. Catalogue no. 4613.0. Australian Bureau of Statistics, Canberra.

Alkire, S. (2002a). Dimensions of human development. *World Development, 30*(2), 181-205. Doi 10.1016/ S0305-750x(01)00109-7

Alkire, S. (2002b). *Valuing Freedoms: Sen's Capability Approach and Poverty Reduction*. Oxford University Press.

Corn, A., & Gumbula, N. (2001). Ancestral precedent as creative inspiration: the influence of soft sands on popular song composition in Arnhem land. In G. K. Ward & A. Muckle (Eds.), *'The power of knowledge, the resonance of tradition'. Electronic publication of papers from the AIATSIS conference, September 2001* (pp. 31-68). Published by the Australian Institute of Aboriginal and Torres Strait Inlander Studies, Canberra.

Costanza, R., d' Arge, R., de Groot, R., Farber, S., Grasso, M., Hannon, B., ... van den Belt, M. (1997). The value of the world's ecosystem services and natural capital. *Nature, 387*, 253-260.

Costanza, R., & Daly, H. E. (1987). Toward an ecological economics. *Ecological Modelling, 38*(1–2), 1-7. doi: http://dx.doi.org/10.1016/0304-3800(87)90041-X

Costanza, R., Fisher, B., Ali, S., Beer, C., Bond, L., Boumans, R., … Snapp, R. (2007). Quality of life: An approach integrating opportunities, human needs, and subjective well-being. *Ecological Economics, 61*(2–3), 267-276. doi: http://dx.doi.org/10.1016/j.ecolecon.2006.02.023

Costanza, R., Ida Kubiszewski, Enrico Giovannini, Hunter Lovins, Jacqueline McGlade, Kate E. Pickett, … Wilkinson, R. (2014). Development: Time to leave GDP behind. *Nature, 505*(7483), 283-285.

Cribb, A. B., & Cribb, J. W. (1975). *Wild food in Australia*. Fontana, Sydney.

Cribb, A. B., & Cribb, J. W. (1981). *Wild medicine in Australia*. Fontana, Sydney.

Cribb, A. B., & Cribb, J. W. (1982). *Useful wild plants in Australia*. Fontana, Sydney.

Daily, G. C. (1997). *Nature's services: societal dependence on natural ecosystems*. Island Press, Washington, D. C., USA.

Daly, H. E. (1973). *Toward a steady state economy*. Freeman: San Francisco.

Daly, H. E. (1977). *Steady state economics*. Island Press, USA.

Daly, H. E. (1991). *Steady State Economics: Second Edition*. Island Press, USA.

Daly, H. E. (1992). Allocation, distribution, and scale: towards an economics that is efficient, just, and sustainable. *Ecological Economics, 6*(3), 185-193. doi: 10.1016/0921-8009(92)90024-M

Daly, H. E. (1996). *Beyond Growth: The Economics of Sustainable Development*. Beacon Press.

Daly, H. E., & Cobb, J. (1989). *For the common good: Redirecting the Economy Toward Community, the Environment, and a Sustainable Future*. Beacon Press, Boston.

Daly, H. E., & Farley, J. (2004). *Ecological Economics: Principles and Applications*. Island Press, Washington DC.

Daly, H. (2005). Economics in a full world. *Scientific American*(September, 2005), 100-107.

Daly, H. (2013). A further critique of growth economics. *Ecological Economics, 88,* 20-24. doi: http://dx.doi.org/10.1016/j.ecolecon.2013.01.007

Diener, E., & Suh, E. (1997). Measuring quality of life: economic, social, and subjective indicators. *Social Indicators Research, 40,* 189:216.

Dodson, M. (1997). Land Rights and Social Justice. In G. Yunupingu (Ed.), *Our Land is Our Life: Land Rights: Past, Present and Future* (pp. 39-51). University of Queensland Press, St Lucia.

Edwards, W. H. (1988). *An introduction to Aboriginal societies.* Social science press, Australia.

Environment Protection and Heritage Council (EPHC). (2009). National waste overview 2009. Former standing Council on Environment and Water. Environment Protection and Heritage Council, Australia.

FAO (Food and Agriculture Organisation). (2008). Climate change and food security: a Framework document. Food and Agriculture Organization of the United Nations, Rome.

FAO (Food and Agriculture Organisation). (2010a). The State of Food Insecurity in the World: Addressing food insecurity in protracted crises. FAO, the United Nations, Rome.

FAO (Food and Agriculture Organisation). (2010b). Global Forest Resources Assessment — Key Findings. Published by the Food and Agriculture Organisation, the United Nations, Rome.

Fisher, B., Turner, R. K., & Morling, P. (2009). Defining and Classifying Ecosystem Services for Decision Making. *Ecological Economics, 68,* 643-653.

Garnaut, R. (2008). The Garnaut Climate Change Review. Cambridge University Press, p. 65.

Gleadow, R. M., Edwards, E., & Evans, J. R. (2009a). Changes in nutritional value of cyanogenic Trifolium repens at elevated carbon dioxide. *Journal of Chemical Ecology, 35,* 476-478.

Gleadow, R. M., Evans, J. R., McCaffrey, S., & Cavagnaro, T. R. (2009b). Growth and nutritive value of cassava (*Manihot esculenta* Cranz.) are reduced when grown at elevated carbon dioxide. *Plant Biology,* 1-7.

Global Footprint Network and Confederation of Indian Industry. (2008). India's ecological footprint — a business perspective. Published by the Global Footprint Network and Confederation of Indian Industry.

Great Barrier Reef Marine Park Authority. (2009). Outlook report. Published by the Great Barrier Reef Marine Park Authority, Townsville, Qld.

Hennessya, K., Fawcett, R., Kironoa, D., Mpelasokaa, F., Jones, D., Batholsa, J., ... Plummerb, N. (2008). An assessment of the impact of climate change on the nature and frequency of exceptional climatic events. Published by the Australian Government, CSIRO and Bureau of Meteorology.

Human Development Report. (1990). Human Development Report 1990. The United Nations Development Programme (UNDP), Oxford University Press.

Human Development Report. (2009). Human Development Report 2009: Overcoming barriers: Human mobility and development. United Nations Development Programme, UN Plaza, New York, NY 10017, USA.

Human Development Report. (2010). The real wealth of nations: Pathways to human development. The United Nations Development Programme (UNDP), UN.

Human Development Report. (2011). Sustainability and equity: A better future for all. Place The United Nations Development Programme (UNDP), UN.

Human Development Report. (2013). Human Development Report 2013. The rise of the South: Human progress in a diverse world. United Nations Development Programme, UN.

IPCC (Intergovernmental Panel on Climate Change). (2005). Carbon dioxide capture and storage. Cambridge University Press.

IPCC (Intergovernmental Panel on Climate Change). (2013). Climate Change 2013: The Physical Science Basis. Summary for policy makers: A report by Working Group I of the Intergovernmental Panel on Climate Change. Published by the IPCC.

IPCC (Intergovernmental Panel on Climate Change). (2014). Climate Change 2014: Synthesis Report. Synthesis Report, IPCC.

Isaacs, J. (1987). *Bush food: Aboriginal food and herbal medicine.* Ure Smith Press, Sydney: Weldon.

Jean, C. (1995). *Biodiversity and intellectual property rights: implications for Indigenous peoples.* Paper presented at the Ecopolitics IX conference: Perspectives on Indigenous peoples management of the environmental resources. Darwin: Northern Land Council.

Keen, I. (2004). *Aboriginal Economy and Society.* Oxford Press.

Lassak, E. V., & McCarthy, T. (1983). *Australian medicinal plants.* Methuen, North Ryde, NSW.

Levitt, D. (1981). *Plants and people: Aboriginal use of plants on Groote Eylandt.* Australian institute of Aboriginal Studies, Canberra.

Low, T. (1989). *Bush tucker — Australian wild food harvest.* Angus and Robertson.

Millennium Ecosystem Assessment. (2003). Ecosystems and Human Well-being: A Framework for Assessment. Island Press, Washington, D.C.

Millennium Ecosystem Assessment. (2005a). *Ecosystems and human well-being: biodiversity synthesis.* World Resources Institute, Washington, D.C.

Millennium Ecosystem Assessment. (2005b). *Ecosystems and human well-being: Synthesis.* Island press, Washington, D.C.

Millennium Ecosystem Assessment (Ed.). (2005c). *Ecosystems and human well-being: Scenarios, Volume 2.* Island Press.

Millennium Ecosystem Assessment (Ed.). (2005d). *Ecosystems and Human well-being: current state and trends, Volume 1.* Island Press.

Millennium Ecosystem Assessment (Ed.). (2005e). *Ecosystems and human well-being: Multiple assessments, Volume 4.* Island Press.

Millennium Ecosystem Assessment (Ed.). (2005f). *Ecosystems and human well-being: Policy responses, Volume 3.* Island Press.

Muir, K. (1998). The earth has an Aboriginal culture inside: Recognising the cultural value of country. Australian Institute of Aboriginal and Torres Strait Islander Studies, Canberra.

National Waste Report. (2010). National Waste Report 2010. Department of the Environment, Water, Heritage and the Arts, Australian Government.

Oke, M., Allan, P., Goldsworthy, K., & Pickin, J. (2009). Waste and Recycling in Australia, 2009– A report prepared by Hyder Consulting for the Department of Environment, Water, Heritage and the Arts, Australia.

Oxford Economics. (2009). Valuing the effects of Great Barrier Reef bleaching. Published by the Great Barrier Reef Foundation, Australia.

Prime Minister's Science, Engineering and Innovation Council. (2010). *Australia and Food Security in a Changing World.* The Prime Minister's Science, Engineering and Innovation Council, Canberra, Australia.

Sangha, K. (2014). Modern agricultural practices and analysis of socioeconomic and ecological impacts of development in agriculture sector, Punjab, India — a review. *Indian Journal of Agricultural Research, 48* (5), 331-341. doi: 10.5958/0976-058X.2014.01312.2

Sen, A. (1981). *Poverty and Famines: An Essay on Entitlement and Deprivation.* Oxford University Press, UK.

Sen, A. (1985). *Commodities and Capabilities.* Amsterdam. North-Holland.

Sen, A. (1993). Capability and wellbeing. In M. Nussbaum & A. Sen (Eds.), *The Quality of Life.* Oxford: Clarendon Press.

Sen, A. (1999a). *Development as Freedom.* Oxford University Press.

Sen, A. (1999b). *Commodities and Capabilities.* Oxford University Press.

Sivadas, E., Bruvold, N. T., & Nelson, M. R. (2008). A reduced version of the horizontal and vertical individualism and collectivism scale: A four-country assessment. *Journal of Business Research, 61,* 201-210.

State of the Environment Committee. (2011). Australia state of the environment 2011. An independent report to the Australian Government, Minister for Sustainability, Environment, Water, Population and Communities (DSEWPaC). Canberra.

State of Climate. (2012). *State of the Climate.* Published by the Bureau of Meteorology and CSIRO (Commonwealth Scientific and Industrial Research Organisation), Australia.

State of Climate. (2014). *State of the Climate.* Published by the Bureau of Meteorology and CSIRO (Commonwealth Scientific and Industrial Research Organisation), Australia.

Strang, V. (2000). Showing and telling: Australian land rights and material moralities. *Journal of Material Culture, 5*(3), 275:299.

The Living Planet Report. (2008). The Living Planet Report 2008. Published by the World Wide Fund for nature (WWF) International.

The Living Planet Report. (2014). The Living Planet Report 2014. Species and Spaces, People and Places. Published by the World Wide Fund for nature (WWF) International.

The United Nations. (2011). *Sustainable development — Harmony with Nature. UN General Assembly Report (A/66/302).* UN, General Assembly 66th Session.

The United Nations. (2011). *Sustainable development — Harmony with Nature. UN General Assembly Report (A/66/204).* UN, General Assembly 66th Session.

Williams, N. M. (1998). CINCRM Discussion Paper no. 1. Intellectual property and Aboriginal environmental knowledge. Centre for Indigenous Natural & Cultural Resource Management, NTU.

World Happiness Report (by Helliwell, J., Layard, R., & Sachs, J.). (2012). World Happiness Report 2012. Published by the Columbia University Earth Institute. Retrieved 29 June 2014.

World Resources 2000-2001. (2000). A guide to World Resources 2000-2001: People and ecosystems: The fraying web of life. World Resources Institute, Washington, DC, USA.

World Resources Institute. (2010-2011). Decision Making in a Changing Climate—Adaptation Challenges and Choices. World Resources Institute (WRI) in collaboration with United Nations Development Programme, United Nations Environment Programme, and World Bank, 2011, Washington, DC.

Web sources:

Alliance for religions and conservation. (2012). http://www.arcworld.org. Retrieved September, 12, 2012-13.

Australian Broadcasting Corporation. (2010). Cyclone Larry: http://www.abc.net.au/am/content/2007/s1876516.htm. Retrieved 7 March, 2012.

Australian Broadcasting Corporation. (2012). Toxic crops: http//http://www.abc.net.au/catalyst/stories/2891924.htm. Retrieved 6 May, 2012.

Bureau Of Meteorology (BOM). http://www.bom.gov.au. Retrieved 21 September, 2012, several times in 2013 and 2014.

Department of the Environment, Australia. (2014). Australia's national biodiversity hotspots: http://www.environment.gov.au/biodiversity/conservation/hotspots/national-biodiversity-hotspots, Retrieved 15 August, 2014.

Ecological footprint calculator. (2012). http://www.wwf.org.au/footprint/calculator. Retrieved 11 December, 2012

Global Footprint Network — Ecological Footprint. (2012 and 2014). http://www.footprintnetwork.org/en/index.php/GFN/page/calculator
Retrieved in 2012 and 2014 (several times).

Further readings:

ABS (2005). *Measures of Australia's progress: summary indicators, 2005.* ABS catalogue no. 1383.0.55.001, Australian Bureau of Statistics, Canberra.

Australian Institute of Aboriginal and Torres Strait Islander Studies. (1994). Land, Rights, Laws: Issues of Native Title: Issue paper no. 3 (Ed. Mary Edmunds). Published by the Australian Institute of Aboriginal and Torres Strait Islander Studies, Canberra.

CAEPR (Centre for Aboriginal Economic Policy Research). (2012). *People on country, healthy landscapes and indigenous economic futures.* Published by CAEPR, The Australian National University, Canberra ACT.

Dodson, M., & McCarthy, D. (2005). Customary Land as the Key for Future Development — empower those who want to use their land and protect those who don't. *The National Land Summit — PNG University of Technology.* 23-25 August 2005 at Lae, PNG.

FAO (Food and Agriculture Organisation). (2001). State of the world's forests 2001. Published by the Food and Agriculture Organisation of the United Nations, Rome.

Jalota, R. K., Sangha, K. K., & Kehal, H. S. (2006). *Sustainable development: state of agriculture and natural resources in Punjab.* Research and Publishing House. New Delhi.

Kaur, K. (2006). The role of ecosystem services from tropical savannas in the well-being of Aboriginal people: A scoping study. A report for the Tropical Savannas Cooperative Research Centre, Darwin, NT.

Kaur, K., & Stanley, O. (2006). *Linking ecosystem services to human well-being: A case study of Aboriginal people in north Australia.* Paper presented at the ISEE (International Society of Ecological Economics) Conference "Ecological sustainability and human well-being", 16-18 Dec, 2006, held at New Delhi, India.

Strang, V. (1997). *Uncommon Ground: Cultural Landscapes and Environmental Values.* Oxford, U.K.; New York: Berg Publishers.

The United Nations Development Programme. (1990 onwards). Human Development Reports. Oxford University Press.

Williams, N. M. (1986). *The Yolngu and their land: A system of land tenure and the fight for its recognition.* Standford University Press.